WEIRD AND
MYSTERIOUS STORIES

THE **G**LOBE **R**EADER'S **C**OLLECTION

WEIRD AND MYSTERIOUS STORIES

ANN ELWOOD

GLOBE BOOK COMPANY
A Division of Simon & Schuster
Englewood Cliffs, New Jersey

ANN ELWOOD is a graduate of Fairleigh Dickinson University. She has taught extensively in both New York and New Jersey school systems. Since 1958 she has worked in educational publishing. Currently Ms. Elwood is both a freelance writer and educational consultant living on the West Coast. She is the author of Globe's *Legends for Everyone, Points of View,* and *Something True, Something Else.*

PHOTO AND ILLUSTRATIONS CREDITS:

Cover Art: James Ennis Kirkland
Cover Design: Marek Antoniak

ISBN: 0-83590-198-0

Printed in the United States of America.
10   9   8   7

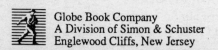

Globe Book Company
A Division of Simon & Schuster
Englewood Cliffs, New Jersey

CONTENTS

UNIT 2 CREATURES: REAL AND IMAGINED

UNIT 3 ADVENTURES INTO THE UNKNOWN

UNIT 4 THE POWER OF MIND, MEDICINE, AND MAGIC

INTRODUCTION

The stories in this book come from many parts of the world. Some of the stories report events that really happened. Others are tales about strange events that somebody, someplace, said happened. The truth of some of these weird tales would be hard to prove. Yet, people love mysteries and that is what Weird and Mysterious is about. It contains articles about mysterious, believe-it-or-not happenings all over the world.

The book is divided into four units. Unit 1 is called "Ghosts and Spirits." Here you will read about the ghost that haunts the White House, the ghost of a Voodoo leader, and a ghost that was actually photographed. In Unit 2 you will read about "Creatures: Real and Imagined." Some of the creatures have been seen by people but never captured or examined; others are real animals that have strange habits. In Unit 3 you will be taken on "Adventures into the Unknown" and will read about places like Zimbabwe (the lost city in Africa) and people like Cinque, who captured a slave ship. In Unit 4 you are told of "The Powers of Mind, Medicine, and Magic." You will read about fire walkers, medicine men, and people like Houdini.

Following each story are activities that will help you sharpen your thinking, improve your reading, and help you develop your vocabulary and writing ability.

unit
1

GHOSTS
and
SPIRITS

1

LINCOLN'S GHOST

PLACES

Holland [HAW-lund] a country in northern Europe

Illinois [il-uh-NOY] a state in the middle of the United States

PEOPLE

Andrew Johnson [AN-droo JAWN-sun] the seventeenth President of the United States

Abraham Lincoln [AY-bruh-ham LINK-un] the sixteenth President of the United States

Eleanor Roosevelt [EL-uh-nor ROHZ-uh-velt] the wife of the thirty-second United States President, Franklin D. Roosevelt

EVENT

Civil War [SIV-ul WOR] a war fought from 1860 to 1865 by one part of the United States against another part

WORDS

coffin [CAW-fin] a box in which a dead person is put

frock coat [FRAWK KOTE] a type of man's coat that was popular about 100 years ago

haunt [HAWNT] visit or live in as a ghost

skeletons [SKEL-un-tinz] the bones of people or animals that make a framework for the body

steam engine [STEEM EN-jun] an engine run by steam

3

There are many stories about ghosts haunting the White House, where Presidents of the United States live. The ghost of one President's wife is said to hang up her ghostly wash in the East Room, as she did when alive. Some people who sleep in Andrew Johnson's bed get chills and hear weird laughter. But the ghost who is said to haunt the White House most is Abraham Lincoln.

Abraham Lincoln went to bed late one night. When he fell asleep, he had a bad dream. In the dream, there was a "deathlike stillness" about him. He heard quiet sobs. It was as though many people were weeping. He left his bed and went downstairs. There he heard more weeping, but he saw no people. From room to room he went. All the rooms had enough light for him to see there was no one in them. Yet there was that crying sound, as if hearts were breaking. When he came to the East Room, he saw a dead body in a coffin. The dead person's face was covered. Lincoln was puzzled. What did it mean? Near the coffin were soldiers acting as guards.

Lincoln asked one of the guards, "Who is that?"

"The President. He was killed," the guard answered.

The crowd broke into louder sobs. Then Lincoln woke up. The dream scared him so much that he did not sleep again that night. Later, for three nights in a row, he dreamed he was going to die. On the fourth night, he went to see a play with his wife. While he was watching it, a gunman came up behind him and shot him. Lincoln died the next morning.

His body was put in a coffin. The coffin was taken on a

slow train to Illinois, where Lincoln came from. The whole country wept for him. He had taken the United States through a Civil War. He had freed blacks from being slaves.

Since then, some people say Lincoln haunts the White House. They think he still cares about what happens to the country. The night before trouble comes, they say he can be heard pacing up and down in the room that was his office. Some people think they can see him staring out a window, as he did in life. His ghost is tall, like him. It is dressed in a frock coat and top hat.

One night, the Queen of Holland was visiting at the White House. A knock came on her bedroom door. She opened it. She thought she saw Lincoln's ghost. The queen passed out. In the morning, when she woke up, she found herself lying on the floor.

A woman who worked for Mrs. Eleanor Roosevelt thought she saw Lincoln, too. She said he was sitting on a bed putting on his boots in one of the rooms. She came out of the room crying and afraid. Mrs. Roosevelt herself said she did not believe in ghosts. But she had heard strange footsteps. And twice, when she was sitting in the room where Lincoln had slept, an odd thing happened. "I'd get a feeling that someone was standing behind me," she said. "I'd have to turn around and look."

Some people have made up a story about ghost trains that come in April, the month Lincoln was killed. They are pulled by old-time steam engines. They travel on the tracks his funeral train followed. First, about midnight, one train passes. There is no noise. Long black ribbons fly in the wind. A band of skeletons sitting on a flat car plays funeral songs. Clouds come over the moon. Then the funeral train itself comes. It, too, flies ribbons. Flags flap. The train rushes past. The tracks seem quiet, as though covered with a rug. A coffin lies in the center of one flat car. There are those who say clocks stop when the trains go by.

READING QUESTIONS

Choose the best answer. Write in your notebook the number of each question and the letter—a, b, c, or d—that shows the best answer.

1. What is this story mostly about?
    (a) A band of skeletons
    (b) Ghosts in the White House
    (c) The Civil War
    (d) A strange dream

2. What is the White House?
    (a) A big house in Illinois
    (b) The place where Presidents live
    (c) A house where the Queen of Holland lives
    (d) A place for dead people

2   What happens to some people who sleep in Andrew
    hnson's bed?
    (a) They die.
    (b) They get chills and hear weird laughter.
    (c) They fall off.
    (d) They end up crying.

4. What did Lincoln see in his bad dream?
   (a) A body in a coffin
   (b) A ghost train
   (c) The end of the world
   (d) A gunman

5. What happened to Lincoln at the play?
   (a) A ghost came at him.
   (b) He died of a bad heart.
   (c) A guard shot him.
   (d) A gunman shot him.

6. During what war was Lincoln president?
   (a) The War for Independence
   (b) The Civil War
   (c) World War I
   (d) World War II

7. What is Lincoln's ghost supposed to do before trouble comes?
   (a) Pace up and down
   (b) Knock on bedroom doors
   (c) Cry out loud
   (d) Call for help

8. What did the Queen of Holland think she saw?
   (a) Lincoln putting on his boots
   (b) A ghostly railroad train
   (c) Lincoln's ghost
   (d) Andrew Johnson's ghost

WORDS TO KNOW

Choose the word that best fits the blank in each sentence. Write it in your notebook beside the number of the sentence.

coffin   frock coat   haunt   skeletons   steam engine

1. Many ghosts are said to _____ the White House.

2. The dead body was put in a _____ .

3. A _____ pulled the train.

4. Lincoln wore a _____ and a top hat.

5. The _____ were made up of bones.

SPEAKING AND LISTENING

Discuss these questions with your classmates.

1. Can dreams tell what will happen in the future? Why do you think so?

2. What is a ghost? Do you believe in ghosts? Why?

3. How might a person prove that ghosts really haunt places? How might a person prove that they don't? Which would be harder to prove? Why?

4. Why are some people afraid of ghosts?

5. Sometimes a person might hear strange sounds at night and think she or he hears a ghost. What real things might make strange sounds at night?

TIME LINE

| 1800 | 1850 | 1900 | 1950 | 1980 |

Copy this time line on a piece of paper. Note that each vertical line means another ten-year period. Now look up the dates when the following people were President of the United States: Andrew Johnson, Abraham Lincoln, Franklin Delano Roosevelt. You can find the dates in a World Almanac or an encyclopedia or an American history book. Write the names of the three Presidents where they belong on the time line.

WRITING ABOUT DREAMS

On a piece of paper, write three sentences that tell about a dream you had. If you can't remember one, make one up. Now write one more sentence telling what you think the dream means.

2

MARIE LEVEAU

PLACE

New Orleans [NOO OR-leenz] a large city in Louisiana

PEOPLE AND ANIMALS

Marie Leveau [muh-REE luh-VOH] a woman who lived in
New Orleans

French [FRENCH] from the country of France, in Europe

Elmore Banks [EL-morh BANKS] a man from New
Orleans

Zombi [ZAHM-bee] a snake

WORDS

Bayou [BIE-yoo] a slow-moving body of water
graveyard [GRAYV-yard] a place where dead people are buried
gris-gris [GREE-GREE] a bag of magic objects
rites [REITS] set ways of doing something
voodoo [VOO-DOO] a religion that uses spells and magic

New Orleans was a lively city 150 years ago. (It is lively now, too.) Many people who lived there were French. Many were black. Others, like Marie Leveau, were part French and part black. Marie was a voodoo leader. What is voodoo? It is a religion that uses spells and magic. Marie was good at it. She may be good at it yet.

Marie Leveau, the voodoo leader, sold gris-gris. Gris-gris is a magic mix. In Marie's famous gris-gris there were dried frogs, bones, dirt from a graveyard, and cats' eyes. People thought that a small black bag of Marie's gris-gris would keep away evil. Marie also made up spells, and she took spells away. She mixed drinks that were supposed to make people fall in love.

All sorts of people came to see Marie. Slaves and rich people came. People who wanted to get even with someone came. People who wanted someone to love them came. People who wanted to get rid of evil spells came. In her house, people saw weird things. There were black cats, spiders, and bats. There was a 20-foot snake called Zombi. He lived on melon and blood. Behind closed doors there were bones of dead people.

Voodoo was against the law in New Orleans. But Marie knew how to get around that. When police came to break up voodoo rites, she could handle them. She talked some into going away. Others took part in what was going on. The ones

who gave her trouble were in for trouble themselves. She could make them get down on the ground and bark like dogs.

Every St. John's Eve (June 22), Marie and crowds of others went to the secret rites at St. John's Bayou. Fires flamed. Marie danced with Zombi. She killed chickens. She made speeches on a black coffin. After the rites were over, everyone went into the water. Not Marie. Marie walked on the water.

Marie probably died in 1881. At least that's what the New Orleans paper said. Her daughter, also named Marie, took over the voodoo business.

But there is another story. There are those who say the first Marie was still going strong in the 1890s. It was then, they say, that she went to her last St. John's Eve rites. While she was there, a great wind came up. It swept Marie and the rest

The tombstone of Marie Leveau. It says that she died July 1, 1897 at 62 years, and was a good mother, a good friend and will be missed by those who knew her. The X marks on the stone are put by people to obtain good luck or ward off evil.

of the crowd away. Later, people saw her as a ghost. She was sitting on a log. Another person saw her sitting on a roof singing voodoo songs.

At Marie's grave, believers leave gris-gris, flowers, and money. They make crosses on the stone with bits of brick. And her ghost may still be around. People say she comes back as a snake or as a big dog. Sometimes she appears as a crazy old woman. They say she comes back as a crow that flies through windows of houses and steals gold. The crow's head feathers look like the head cloth Marie wore. The head cloth was tied in seven knots, points up.

A story was told, not long ago, about a man named Elmore Banks who was sitting in a soda shop. He was about to order a soda. Then a woman came in. She was wearing a long white dress. On her head was a cloth tied in seven knots. The man behind the counter ran away when he saw her. Elmore didn't.

"Don't you know who I am?" the woman asked.

"No," said Elmore.

The woman hit him in the face. Then she seemed to float up and out of the shop. She floated past the walls of the graveyard. Elmore was so scared he passed out. When he came to, the owner of the shop told him he had seen and talked to the famous Marie Leveau.

They say Marie still comes back on St. John's Eve. People along the bayou say they hear her singing in the wind. And they say her shape floats on a log in the water.

READING QUESTIONS

Choose the best answer. Write in your notebook the number of each question and the letter—a, b, c, or d—that shows the best answer.

1. What is this story mostly about?
   - (a) New Orleans
   - (b) Marie Leveau
   - (c) St. John's Eve
   - (d) Elmore Banks

2. Who was Marie Leveau?
   - (a) A housewife
   - (b) A voodoo leader
   - (c) A snake
   - (d) A crow

3. What is voodoo?
   - (a) A way of cooking food
   - (b) A way of talking
   - (c) A kind of dance
   - (d) A religion that uses spells and magic

4. What did Zombi live on?
   - (a) Melon and blood
   - (b) Snakes and spiders
   - (c) Gris-gris
   - (d) Rats and mice

5. What did Marie do to police who gave her trouble?
   - (a) She talked them into going away.
   - (b) She fed them gris-gris.
   - (c) She got Zombi to bite them.
   - (d) She made them get on the ground and bark like dogs.

6. Why didn't Marie go into the water after the rites?
   - (a) She was afraid of drowning.
   - (b) She had to stay on shore.
   - (c) She walked *on* it instead.
   - (d) She floated on a log.

7. Why do some people think a crow is Marie's ghost?
   (a) Its voice is like hers.
   (b) Its head feathers look like her head cloth.
   (c) It cannot fly.
   (d) It lives near the graveyard where she is buried.

8. What do people leave on Marie's grave?
   (a) Gris-gris, flowers, and money
   (b) Food and jewels
   (c) Cats' eyes and bones
   (d) Fruit and vegetables

WORDS TO KNOW

Choose the word that best fits the blank in each sentence. Write it in your notebook beside the number of the sentence.

    rites   graveyard   gris-gris   bayou   voodoo

1. Every St. John's Eve, Marie went to the _____ rites at the bayou.
2. People thought that _____ would keep evil away.
3. When Marie died, she was buried in the _____ .
4. At the voodoo _____ , Marie danced with Zombi.
5. As a ghost, Marie floats in the water of the _____ on a log.

DETAILS

In the story, find sentences that answer these questions. Write those sentences on a piece of paper.

1. What is voodoo?
2. What was Marie's gris-gris made of?
3. Why did police break up voodoo rites?

4. Who took over the business after Marie died?

5. What do believers use to make crosses with?

6. What did Marie's head cloth look like?

7. What did Marie do to Elmore Banks?

FINDING IT

Look up New Orleans on a map. Now read about its history. Answer this question in two sentences: Why do many people in New Orleans speak French?

SPEAKING AND LISTENING

Discuss these questions with your classmates.

1. Do you believe in voodoo? Why?

2. Would voodoo work better on people who believe in it? Why?

3. Do you think people might be more likely to get sick if they thought they were going to get sick? Why?

4. What might happen to a person who thinks an evil spell has been cast on him?

5. Do you think Zombi really lived on melon and blood? What makes you say so?

6. Do you think Marie was able to walk on water? What makes you say so?

7. If you think you will do well on a test, do you have a better chance of getting an "A"? Why?

8. If you think you will be happy, will you be happy? Why?

9. How much power do your thoughts have on you? Give an example.

WRITING ABOUT WHAT PEOPLE BELIEVE

Many people think that a black cat means bad luck. Others believe that if you step on a crack in the sidewalk, you will break your mother's back. Think of some odd beliefs you have heard about. Write three of them on a piece of paper. Choose one of these beliefs and write a sentence about it. State whether or not you believe it to be true.

THE BROWN LADY

PLACES

England [ING-lund] a country in western Europe

Raynham Hall [RAYN-um HAWL] a big country house in England

PEOPLE

Colonel Loftus [KERN-ul LAWF-tus] a guest at Raynham Hall

Indre Shira [IND-ruh sher-AH] a man who takes pictures

WORDS

bullets [BUL-uts] pieces of metal made to be shot from a gun

chess [CHES] a game played on a board

genuine [JEN-yoo-in] real

magazine [MAG-uh-zeen] a printed piece containing writings and put out at regular times, perhaps every month

veil [VAYL] a very thin piece of cloth, usually worn over a woman's face

England is a country full of ghost stories. Many of the stories tell of ghosts that haunt rich people's houses. The Brown Lady is one of the ghosts. She "lives" at Raynham Hall, a big country place. No one knows who she was when she was alive.

23

The Brown Lady was first seen in 1835. That winter a group of people came to spend a week or two at Raynham Hall. It was like a very long party.

One night, Colonel Loftus, one of the guests, played chess with another guest. The game was so interesting that it went on for a long time. It was after midnight when the two men set off for bed. Upstairs, they saw a figure moving down the hall. The figure's footsteps made no sound. The two men could tell that it was a woman. She wore a brown dress. She faded away to nothing. So she had to be a ghost.

Later that week, Loftus saw the Brown Lady again. This time he ran after her to get a closer look. Face to face with her, he got a shock. Her face was lit with a strange light. And there were holes where the eyes should be. Again she faded away like smoke.

Loftus drew a quick picture of the Brown Lady. The owners of Raynham Hall said she had been seen before. They had a better picture made from the one Loftus had drawn. It was hung in the room where Loftus had slept.

Years later, a writer guest asked to stay in that room. He wanted to prove that the Brown Lady story was nonsense. One night, carrying a hunting gun he had gotten from another room, he came down the hall. With him were two other guests. Then they saw the Brown Lady. She had a lamp in her hand. Her face was the same as the one in the picture hanging on the wall in the writer's room. Scared, he fired the gun. The bullets went right through the ghost and into the door of the room across the way. The ghost kept walking.

In 1928, the owner of Raynham Hall asked Indre Shira to come there. Shira was a photographer, and the owner wanted some pictures of the place. At four in

the afternoon, Shira was standing by the stairs with his helper. The helper was putting a plate in the camera. Shira held the flash gun. They were getting ready to take shots. Then Shira saw something. It was near the top of the stairs where the helper couldn't see. Shira later said that the something looked like a cloud at first. Then it slowly turned into the shape of a woman covered with a veil. She started floating down the steps.

"Take a picture!" Shira shouted to the helper.

The helper took the shot. Shira fired the flash.

Then the helper said, "What is this all about?"

Shira told him what he had seen. There had been a figure floating down the stairs, he said. You could see right through it. The helper didn't believe him. He laughed.

"I bet the photograph will show something," Shira said. He was right. The picture showed what looks like a ghost. The photograph appeared in a magazine in 1936. Experts said it was not faked.

One ghost hunter says, "It may well be the only genuine ghost photograph we have."

READING QUESTIONS

Choose the best answer. Write in your notebook the number of each question and the letter—a, b, c, or d—that shows the best answer.

1. What is the most important thing that happens in this story?
    (a) Colonel Loftus sees a ghost.
    (b) A writer shoots at a ghost.
    (c) Indre Shira takes a ghost's picture.
    (d) A ghost is first seen at Raynham Hall.

2. What did Loftus see the second time he ran into the Brown Lady?
    (a) That she wore no clothes
    (b) That she had no eyes
    (c) That she wore a brown dress
    (d) That she was really a man

3. How did the owners of Raynham Hall know what Loftus saw?
    (a) He drew a picture of the Brown Lady.

   (b) They were with him when he saw the Brown Lady.

   (c) They took his word for it.

   (d) He brought the Brown Lady down to see them.

4. Why did the writer want to stay in Loftus's room?

   (a) He wanted to prove the story was nonsense.

   (b) He wanted to write about the Brown Lady.

   (c) He was afraid of the Brown Lady.

   (d) He liked the view.

5. What did the writer do when he saw the Brown Lady?

   (a) He cried out loudly.

   (b) He shot her.

   (c) He drew her picture.

   (d) He called for help.

6. Why did Shira come to Raynham Hall?

   (a) To find the ghost

   (b) To go to a party

   (c) To see the owner

   (d) To take pictures

7. Why didn't Shira's helper see the ghost?

   (a) He was taking pictures.

   (b) He didn't believe in ghosts.

   (c) He was in a place where he couldn't see her.

   (d) He had been blinded by the flash.

8. What did the photograph show?

   (a) What looks like a ghost

   (b) Nothing but stairs

   (c) Indre Shira

   (d) The helper

WORDS TO KNOW

Choose the word that best fits the blank in each sentence. Write it in your notebook beside the number of the sentence.

bullets   chess   genuine   magazine   veil

1. A _____ hung over her face.

2. The photograph was _____ .

3. The _____ had been shot from a gun.

4. Loftus liked to play games of _____ .

5. The photograph was shown in a _____ .

SPEAKING AND LISTENING

Discuss these questions with your classmates.

1. How might a photograph of a ghost be faked?

2. Do you think Shira's photograph shows a real ghost? Why?

3. How are special effects done on television? In movies? Tell about three examples of special effects you have seen.

4. What might ghost hunters do in order to find a ghost?

5. What would you do to find out if a ghost story were true?

DRAWING

On a piece of paper, draw a picture of the Brown Lady as Loftus saw her. Reread the story to get the details right.

WRITING A STORY

Make up a ghost story. Or, write your own version of a ghost story you have heard.

4

THE WYNYARD GHOST

PEOPLE

John Sherbroke [JAWN SHER-bruk] ⎫
George Wynyard [JORJ WIN-yerd] ⎬ soldiers in Canada
⎭

WORDS

message [MES-ij] something told to someone in writing, talking, or some other way

telegraph [TEL-uh-graf] a way of sending messages over wires using a code of dots and dashes

telephone [TEL-uh-fohn] a way of sending people's voices over wires

In the year 1785, John Sherbroke and George Wynyard were soldiers in Canada. Canada was an ocean away from their home in England. At that time Canada belonged to England. English soldiers had to guard it. In those days there were no fast ships or planes or telegraphs or telephones. It took weeks for a message or a person to cross the ocean.

The winter night was cold. George Wynyard was studying in one of his two rooms. With him was his friend John Sherbroke. A candle burned on the table. Suddenly, they saw a strange sight. It was a young man. He was skinny and pale as death. His clothes were thin, no good for cold nights. On his head was a round hat.

George Wynyard turned white. He and the figure stared at each other. The figure stood there quietly for a few minutes. His face was sad and loving. Then he passed between the two men and went into the inner room.

"Who's that?" asked John.

"Why, that was my brother!" answered George. "I'm sure he is dead." It was all he could think of. He knew his brother was in England. There was no way for him to have gotten to Canada. So for him to show up meant that he was a ghost.

"Your brother? What do you mean? There must be some trick," said John. Then he made a joke. He could see his friend was upset. "The fellow has a good hat. I wish I had it." Hats like the ghost wore were hard to come by in Canada. The one John had was worn out.

With another soldier, the two went into the inner room. No one was there. Yet how could the figure have gotten out? The room had no door to the outside. All the windows were shut tight. The figure had not gone back through the door into the outer room. It must have faded away. So it must have been a ghost. George wept. Now he was sure his brother was dead.

Both men wrote down what had happened and when. George was very worried. He wrote a letter to England. In it he asked for news of his brother.

Five months later, an answer came. It came to John, not George. A doctor soldier wrote the letter. John got it when he and George were about to eat dinner in the big hall. John opened the letter and read the first few lines. It began, "Dear John, Break to your friend Wynyard the death of his brother. . . "

Quietly John led George outside and told him what the letter said. Then, leaving his friend alone, he came back into

the dining hall. He said to the man next to him, "Wynyard's brother is dead!"

The letter had told more. It told the time the brother had died. It was when the figure had come to George's room.

READING QUESTIONS

Choose the best answer. Write in your notebook the number of each question and the letter—a, b, c, or d—that shows the best answer.

1. What is this story mostly about?
   (a) A ghost that visited a brother
   (b) Ghosts of people in other countries
   (c) Beliefs some people have about ghosts
   (d) Ghosts that haunt houses

2. Where was George Wynyard in 1785?
   (a) The United States
   (b) England
   (c) Canada
   (d) Europe

3. What time of the year was it when George saw a ghost?
   (a) Winter
   (b) Summer
   (c) Spring
   (d) Fall

4. Where was George's brother supposed to be?
   (a) At sea
   (b) In England
   (c) In Canada
   (d) In India

5. What happened to the ghost?
   (a) It went into the inner room and disappeared.
   (b) It left through the window.
   (c) It left through the door.
   (d) It broke the window.

6. What did George and John write down?
   (a) The ghost's name
   (b) What happened and when
   (c) The words the ghost said
   (d) The fear they felt

7. Why did George write to England?
   (a) To find out about his brother
   (b) To ask for news of his father
   (c) To see when he could come home
   (d) To ask for news of his mother

8. How did George find out his brother had died?
   (a) A doctor wrote to John.
   (b) His mother wrote to him.

(c) His father wrote to him.

(d) John wrote to him.

WORDS TO KNOW

Choose the word that best fits the blank in each sentence. Write it in your notebook beside the number of the sentence.

telephone   telegraph   message

1. You can send a _____ over the telegraph.

2. If you want to call your friend, you pick up the _____ and dial.

3. You can send a message by _____ through Western Union.

SPEAKING AND LISTENING

Discuss these questions with your classmates.

1. How did George and John decide the figure was a ghost?

2. What clues told them the ghost was from England, not Canada?

3. Why did John make the joke about the hat?

4. How did they know the ghost had faded away?

5. Why might the doctor have written to John, not George?

6. Why was it important that the two men wrote something when they saw the ghost?

7. This ghost, if it *was* a ghost, showed up in 1785. How long ago was that? What if you heard about a ghost that showed up last year? Would you believe that story more than the one about the Wynyard ghost? Why?

WRITING A LETTER

Finish writing the letter from the doctor. You might want to make up something about how the brother died.

5

THE POLTERGEIST

PLACE

Florida [FLAHR-uh-dah] a state in the southern
United States

PERSON

Julio Vasquez [HOO-lee-oh vas-KEZ] a young man with
strange powers

WORDS

alligator [AL-uh-gay-ter] a big animal that looks like a snake
with legs

cause [CAWZ] a reason; what makes something happen

dice [DICE] cubes marked with one to six spots and used to
play a game

polish [PAH-lish] something used to make something else shine
poltergeist [POHL-ter-giest] a noisy ghost
stock boy [STAWK BOI] a person who keeps things in order and
puts things on shelves

Poltergeist means "noisy ghost." Some people think that a poltergeist takes over a young person. It lives inside the person, and the person gives the poltergeist power. Others think there is no "ghost" at all. Anything the young person does, she or he does alone. Odd things happen when a poltergeist is around. Objects fly off shelves. They are thrown across a room. All this happens when no one is close to the objects.

At first it was just a day like any other that year of 1967. Down at the workshop, people were making gift items. Painters were painting pictures on ashtrays. Workers were putting boxes on shelves. Then the place went crazy. Boxes fell off shelves. Ashtrays flew around the room. It was as if someone unseen were pushing and throwing things. But no one was close enough to have done it.

One of the painters said, "Just a little while ago, I was talking to Julio when I saw a big cardboard box on top of a shelf start to move by itself. It fell down. I ran away screaming and crying." Julio Vasquez, the person she talked to, was a worker there. He was nineteen years old. Every time something fell, his heart pounded.

People came to watch when they heard about the poltergeist. (That's what everyone said was doing the throwing.) The police came, too. One police officer called his boss and said, "You'd better come over here. There's something mighty strange going on."

"Well," the boss said, "can't you save me a trip and tell me about it over the phone?"

"No, said the police officer. "I can't."

The poltergeist was smart. When you looked one place, things fell in another. Once men with TV cameras came to get a picture of something flying. They waited for hours. Nothing happened. At last they gave up. When they had packed up, things started flying again. They never did get a picture.

Police and other experts ruled out causes for what was going on. The cause wasn't a boom from a fast plane. It wasn't a gas leak or water running under the ground. The fans did not blow air strongly enough to push boxes off shelves. Was it a trick using string, ice, or wires? They ruled that out, too.

Julio was the center. Things fell mostly when he was around. If there was a poltergeist, it was inside Julio. Some thought the poltergeist was Lisa, a monkey who had died. She had belonged to an owner of the workshop. Throwing things had been one of her sports. She liked getting in people's hair. The last thing she had done was smash an egg on her owner's head.

During a few days in late January, things went even crazier. Everything fell and flew: glasses and bottles, a nut carved like a head, a bell, a whole box of glasses, a drawer full of little nails.

The owners were sick of it. They brought in a man who knew magic to get rid of the poltergeist. The man shaped leaves into circles. He put the leaves in special places. On a shelf he put a toy alligator. Then he piled toys up. "Look, these are for you to play with," he said to the poltergeist. "Leave everything else alone." It worked. Nothing happened for two days. But people missed the poltergeist. They took away what the man had set up. In an hour an ashtray fell. The people cheered at the sight.

At last the owners had had enough. They were losing money. So they fired Julio. With him went the poltergeist.

Some experts thought that Julio was not haunted by a ghost at all. Their ideas was this. Julio was angry at the owners of the workshop. He held his feelings in. But his mind got the better of him. It was so strong that he could move things with its power alone. He didn't know he was doing it, though. These people tested Julio. They found he could, with his mind alone, make a number come up on dice.

Julio had other jobs after that. One was at a shoe store. While he was there, bottles of shoe polish flew across the room. They even flew around corners. His next job was as a stock boy. Again weird things happened. Cups fell into pieces. Bottles blew up.

Julio is older now. Strange things don't happen as much. But his wife says he still has the power. Once, during an argument, she was almost hit by a glass that flew out of nowhere.

READING QUESTIONS

Choose the best answer. Write in your notebook the number of each question and the letter—a, b, c, or d—that shows the best answer.

1. What is this story mostly about?
   (a) How some strange things were blamed on a ghost
   (b) How people are afraid of ghosts
   (c) How people go about getting rid of ghosts
   (d) How the ghost of a monkey caused trouble

2. According to the story, what happens when a poltergeist is around?
   (a) The room gets dark.
   (b) Things fly around.
   (c) People can't speak.
   (d) Time stops.

3. What did the owners do first to get rid of the poltergeist?
   (a) They brought in a man who knew magic.
   (b) They fired Julio.
   (c) They got rid of Lisa.
   (d) They talked to Julio.

4. What did the man who knew magic do?
   (a) He piled toys up.
   (b) He told Julio to quit what he was doing.
   (c) He moved things on the shelves.
   (d) He bought a pet monkey.

5. What did the owners finally do?
   (a) They called in experts.
   (b) They got rid of the monkey.
   (c) They fired Julio.
   (d) They yelled at the man who knew magic.

6. What did some experts think about Julio and the poltergeist?

    (a) What happened had no cause.
    (b) A strange ghost was inside Julio.
    (c) Julio's anger made things happen.
    (d) Julio knew magic.

7. How did experts test Julio?
    (a) They asked him to make a bottle move.
    (b) They put him in a room with bottles.
    (c) They told him he had no magic.
    (d) They asked him to make a number come up on dice.

8. How do we know Julio may still have the power to move things with his mind?
    (a) Experts say so.
    (b) His wife says so.
    (c) His friends say so.
    (d) He says so.

WORDS TO KNOW

Choose the word that best fits the blank in each sentence. Write it in your notebook beside the number of the sentence.

cause   dice   stock boy   alligator   polish   poltergeist

1. Shoe _____ is used to make shoes shine.

2. People play games with _____ .

3. The man who knew magic put a toy _____ on a shelf.

4. The experts ruled out more than one _____ for what was happening.

5. Julio worked as a _____ .

6. The word _____ means "noisy ghost."

SPEAKING AND LISTENING

Discuss these questions with your classmates.

1. The story tells of two causes for poltergeists. What are

they? Which one sounds like the better answer to the question "What is a poltergeist?" Why? Are there any other answers to that question? If so, what are they?

2. How could you prove that people have the power to move things with their minds? How would you prove that no one has that power?

3. What other poltergeist stories do you know?

CAUSES

When the objects started flying around, experts looked for causes. The causes could have been any of the following:

(a) The boom from a fast plane

(b) A gas leak

(c) Water running under the ground

(d) Fans blowing air strongly enough to push boxes off shelves

(e) A trick

(f) The power of Julio's mind

Think of a cause for each of the following events. Write a sentence about the cause on a piece of paper.

Example:

You break your leg.   Cause: You fell off a stone wall.

1. You get an "A" on a test.

2. A person's car runs out of gas five miles from a station.

3. The room gets too hot for you to work.

4. A plant dies.

5. A friend becomes very angry.

WRITING A PROCEDURE

Work out a way to show how a box could be made to fall off a shelf using one of the following: string, ice, wires. Write up the procedure. Then, demonstrate the trick to the class.

unit
2

CREATURES: REAL and IMAGINED

6

MOTHMAN

PLACES

Point Pleasant [POYNT PLES-unt] a town in West Virginia

West Virginia [WEST ver-JIN-yuh] a state in the southern United States

WORDS

businesspersons [BIZ-uh-nis-pur-sons] people who run or help to run businesses

creature [CREE-cher] an animal

helicopter [HEL-uh-KOP-ter] a flying machine that can lift straight up in the air when it takes off

It all happened in the winter of 1966-67. The place was a town called Point Pleasant. There are those who think the whole town went crazy.

It was 10:30 in the morning. A girl named Connie was driving home from church. Then, beside the road, she said she saw something. It made her put her foot on the brake. There stood a huge gray creature. The creature was seven feet tall and very broad. Later Connie said, "It's a wonder I didn't run off the road and have a wreck."

She slowed down. As she did, wings unfolded from the back of the creature. The wings were ten feet across. The creature rose straight up, like a helicopter. The wings did not flap. It headed for the car. Its red, glowing eyes stared at her. She stepped hard on the gas as the creature swooped low over the car.

This story would not mean much if only Connie saw the creature. But that winter more than 100 others saw it. At first they called it just "Bird." Then someone named it "Mothman." With its wings spread, it did look like a huge moth. So the name stuck.

One night two young couples were driving along the back roads. They saw two red eyes. The eyes were about two inches across and six inches apart. One of the women drew in her breath. The driver slammed on the brakes.

"What is it?" asked someone from the back seat. But no one answered.

Something moved. At first they thought it was an animal. But they knew there was no animal that looked like that. According to them, the creature was about seven feet tall. It was grayish in color. It walked on two legs. Its wings were folded along its back. And its eyes were like huge red reflectors. For a full minute the people in the car stared. They couldn't take their eyes off the creature. Their minds were held by a kind of fear. Then the creature turned away.

"Let's get out of here," one of the people in the car yelled. The driver stepped on the gas and headed for the main road. Then they saw the creature again. It was standing on a hill. It spread its wings and took off—straight up.

"It's following us," someone said. The driver pushed the car to go faster and faster. At 100 miles an hour, the creature was still there. It made a sound like a big mouse.

At the edge of town, the creature stopped following them. The people went to the police station. They told the police what had happened. Some of the police went to the place where the creature had been seen. They found nothing. But when they turned on their police radio, it wouldn't work right. A weird sound came from it. They couldn't get through to the police station.

Mothman was seen many more times: by homemakers, by businesspersons, by two firefighters. Five teenagers saw it standing by a woods. "Nobody believes us because we're teenagers," one said. "But it was really scary." A soldier saw Mothman sitting in a tree like a huge bird. All the people who saw it were taken with cold fear. They had the idea that something wasn't right. Weird feelings went through them.

READING QUESTIONS

Choose the best answer. Write in your notebook the number of each question and the letter—a, b, c, or d—that shows the best answer.

1. What is the most important thing that this story tells?
    (a) More than 100 people saw the creature.
    (b) The creature had red glowing eyes.
    (c) A soldier saw the creature sitting in a tree.
    (d) Weird feelings went through people who saw the creature.

2. When was Mothman seen in Point Pleasant?
    (a) During the winter of 1966
    (b) During the summer of 1966
    (c) During the spring of 1966
    (d) During the fall of 1966

3. How tall was Mothman said to be?
    (a) Three feet
    (b) Ten feet
    (c) Nine feet
    (d) Seven feet

4. How did Mothman fly?
   (a) Like a bird
   (b) Like a helicopter
   (c) Like a plane
   (d) Like a man

5. How big were Mothman's eyes supposed to be?
   (a) Tiny
   (b) Two inches across
   (c) Six inches across
   (d) A half-inch across

6. What color were Mothman's eyes said to be?
   (a) Yellow
   (b) Black
   (c) Gray
   (d) Red

7. What happened to the police who went to look
   for Mothman?
   (a) They saw Mothman.
   (b) They were taken away.
   (c) They took Mothman to the station.
   (d) They couldn't get through to the station
       on the radio.

8. Why didn't some people believe the teen-agers who
   saw Mothman?
   (a) Because people don't always trust teen-agers
   (b) Because the teen-agers were liars
   (c) Because no one knew the teen-agers
   (d) Because the police didn't believe the teen-agers

WORDS TO KNOW

Choose the word that best fits the blank in each sentence. Write it in your notebook beside the number of the sentence.

creature   helicopter   businesspersons   reflectors

1. Mothman was a scary _____.

2. A _____ is a kind of flying machine.

3. Mothman's eyes look like huge red _____ .

4. The _____ ran a place that made helicopters.

SPEAKING AND LISTENING

Discuss these questions with your classmates.

1. Do you believe Mothman was real? Why or why not?

2. Why is it hard to believe that Mothman could fly?

3. What might you do to prove that there is a Mothman?

WRITING TO PERSUADE

Write a few sentences in which you state your reasons for believing Mothman is or is not real. If you believe Mothman is real, what do you think it really is? What makes you think so? Try to be persuasive by citing story details.

7

INSIDE A
FLYING SAUCER

PEOPLE

Barney Hill [BAR-nee HILL] ⎫ people who had a
Betty Hill [BEH-tee HILL] ⎭ strange experience

WORDS

examined [eks-AM-und] looked over closely

strange [STRAINJ] unusual, odd

flying saucer [FLY-ing SAW-sur] an object rhought to be from outer
   space

hypnotized [HIP-noh-tiezd] put into a state like sleep

psychiatrist [sie-KIE-uh-trist] a doctor who helps people who have problems in their personal lives

Betty and Barney Hill tell a strange story. They say they were given a ride in a flying saucer.

On September 19, 1961, Betty and Barney Hill were driving home from Canada when Betty Hill saw something. She thought it was a star. But it kept getting bigger and bigger.

Was it moving? She couldn't tell. Betty pointed the thing out to Barney, her husband. They stopped the car to look at it. They weren't afraid. At least not yet. They drove on.

Then the thing started to move toward them. Barney stopped the car, and the two of them got out.

"It's got to be a plane," Barney said.

"With a crazy course like that?" asked Betty.

Barney said that it might be a small plane carrying lost hunters.

"It's not hunting season," answered Betty. "And I don't hear a sound."

"The wind might be carrying the sound in the other direction," said Barney.

"There is no wind," said Betty.

Now the thing was hanging above the treetops. Its lights flashed red, yellow, green, and blue. Barney started the car and drove along the road. Their dog whined.

The thing came closer. Now Barney and Betty could see its shape. It was like a huge flying saucer. There was a row of

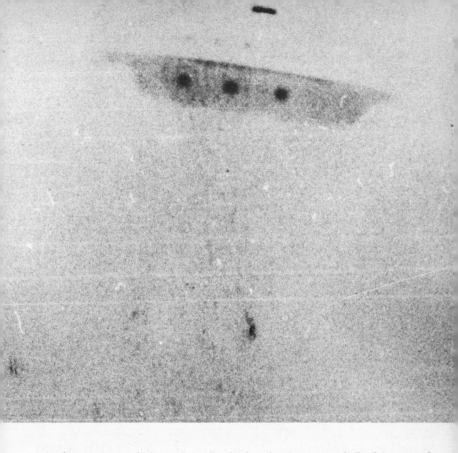

windows around the edge. Its lights had stopped flashing and were glowing white.

Barney brought the car to a stop. The flying saucer landed on the ground. Barney walked toward it. He didn't know why. Something drew him. He felt his body move, but his mind seemed to be separate. Betty called after him, "Barney, come back. Do you hear me?" But he didn't answer.

Inside the ship were beings in black clothes. Barney could see them moving behind the windows. A ladder came down out of the ship. Barney could see one of the beings staring at him. Somehow he knew that the being was telling him not to be afraid. It was talking to him without words. Thoughts were going from its mind to Barney's mind.

The beings were a little shorter than people. Their eyes

were big and wrapped around their heads. They had gray shiny skin. Their noses and mouths were slits. They had no hair.

Betty and Barney were taken into the ship. Both were examined. The beings scraped dry skin from them. They took bits of hair and fingernail. One thing really surprised them. Barney's teeth came out, but Betty's didn't. They asked Betty why that was. She said that people sometimes lost their teeth when they got old.

"Old? What is old?" one asked.

Betty tried to explain. But the beings did not know what a year was, or a day, or an hour.

When it was time to go, the leader told Betty and

Barney to forget what had happened. "I won't forget about it!" said Betty. "I'll remember if it's the last thing I do!"

But she did forget. So did Barney. When they drove home, they remembered seeing the flying ship. But they did not remember going inside it.

Three years later, the two were not feeling happy. Betty was having bad dreams. Things were not going well for Barney. So they went to a psychiatrist. He hypnotized them. It was only then that they remembered being in the ship.

What really happened? Some people think the Hills' story is true. The psychiatrist says they were telling what they thought was the truth. But people can believe strange things when they are hypnotized.

READING QUESTIONS

Choose the best answer. Write in your notebook the number of each question and the letter—a, b, c, or d—that shows the best answer.

1.   What is this story mostly about?
     (a) Two people who say they were taken for a ride in a flying saucer
     (b) A psychiatrist who believes he has seen flying saucers
     (c) A group of people who claim to have come to Earth in a flying saucer
     (d) A flying saucer that has landed several times and been seen by many people

2.   What did Betty say she thought the flying ship was at first?
     (a) A UFO
     (b) A star
     (c) A streetlight
     (d) A plane

3.   How did Barney say the being talked?
     (a) It knew how to speak English.
     (b) It sent thoughts from its mind to his.
     (c) It had a machine that spoke English.
     (d) It used its hands.

4.   What did the Hills say the beings did to them?
     (a) They examined them.
     (b) They asked them questions.
     (c) They hurt them.
     (d) They took them to another world.

5.   What surprised the beings?
     (a) That Betty and Barney had hair
     (b) That they spoke English

(c) That they had fingernails

(d) That Barney's teeth came out

6. When did Betty and Barney say they first remembered what happened?

(a) When the beings told them they could

(b) When a psychiatrist hypnotized them

(c) When it came to them in a dream

(d) When the beings came back

7. What did the psychiatrist think about what happened to the Hills?

(a) That they were crazy

(b) That they saw the flying saucer in a movie

(c) That they dreamed it all

(d) That they were telling what they thought was the truth

8. What can happen to people who are hypnotized?

(a) They can see the future.

(b) They can believe strange things.

(c) They can read minds.

(d) They can fly.

WORDS TO KNOW

Choose the word that best fits the blank in each sentence. Write it in your notebook beside the number of the sentence.

flying saucer   psychiatrist   examined   hypnotized   strange

1. The psychiatrist who _____ Betty and Barney hoped they would remember what happened to them.

2. At first, the _____ looked like a star.

3. The Hills went to see the _____ because they were not feeling well.

4. It was _____ to see an airplane flying so close to the trees.

5. The beings _____ Betty and Barney to see what the Hills were made of.

SPEAKING AND LISTENING

Discuss these questions with your classmates.

1. Why might Barney have wanted to think the flying saucer was a plane?

2. Why do you think the beings took dry skin, fingernails, and hair from the Hills?

3. Why might the beings not know about people's teeth?

4. Why might the beings not know about time?

WHAT IS TRUE

Some things are easier to believe than others. On a piece of paper, write the numbers 1 through 5. For number 1, pick the sentence from the following list that tells about something that is easiest for you to believe. Write it next to number 1. Then choose the sentence that tells about something that is next easiest for you to believe. Write this sentence next to number 2. Keep rating the sentences and writing them next to numbers until you finish number 5. Number 5 should be the sentence telling about the thing you find hardest to believe. Then check all the sentences you think tell about true facts.

1. Betty and Barney Hill were examined by strange beings from outer space.

2. Betty and Barney Hill thought they were telling the truth about what happened to them.

3. Betty and Barney Hill really did see a flying saucer.

4. Betty and Barney Hill went to see a psychiatrist.

5. Betty and Barney Hill are real people.

WRITING A RESPONSE

Choose one of the following questions and then write a couple of sentences to answer it.

1. What language might beings from outer space speak? How might they understand English? How might they make themselves understood?

2. Why do some people want to believe in flying saucers?

3. What might beings from outer space think of cars, school, football games, and television?

8

THREE MYSTERIES ABOUT ANIMALS

PLACES

California [kal-uh-FORN-yuh] a state in the western United States
Mexico [MEKS-uh-koh] a country in North America

WORDS

lemming [LEM-ing] an animal like a rat with a short tail
Monarch [MON-ark] a kind of butterfly
scientists [SIE-un-tists] people who study nature, among
    other things
sponge [SPUHNJ] a sea animal

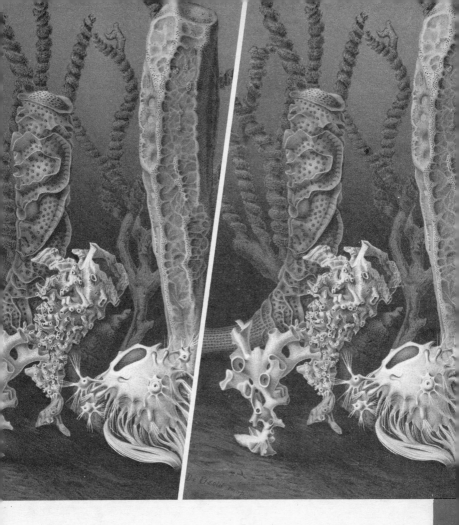

Animals can do things people still can't explain. Here are three animal mysteries. The message? People don't know everything.

THE STRANGE BEHAVIOR OF LEMMINGS

Lemmings are animals that look like rats with short tails. They live in countries where it snows. Because of that, all they can eat in winter are the few plants that grow under the snow. Every few years, they get together in huge groups. Then they start running. They are so close together that they look like a weird, moving rug. Often they step on each other. Foxes, owls, and people kill them. Some groups run until almost all of them drop dead. Others run into the ocean and drown.

People have wondered why lemmings behave this way. Recently, scientists have suggested the following explanation. They say that every few years the number of lemmings grows very large. There is not enough food for all the lemmings. Then they start to move. Huge packs of lemmings keep moving in their search for food. Finally they come to the high cliffs over the ocean. Many lemmings fall over and drown. Soon there are only a few lemmings left. These few lemmings have enough to eat. They turn around and go back. They have babies. Once again,

there will be too many lemmings and they will all start running again.

SPONGES THAT CAN PUT THEMSELVES BACK TOGETHER

Most sponges you buy in a store are models of the skeleton of a real sponge. A real sponge is made up of thousands of little animals. These animals act like one big one. They live on rocks in the ocean.

Sponges can do at least two things people cannot do.

1. A sponge can put itself together. Every sponge has a shape all its own. It has a certain number of holes. Break a sponge into thousands of pieces and put it in a tank. In a day, the pieces will have come together. The new

sponge will be in every way like the old one, holes and all.

2. A sponge can grow a whole new sponge from a piece of itself. Put a piece of a sponge on a rock. It will grow into a whole sponge just like the one it came from. In every part of a sponge, there is a plan of the whole. It's as if a whole person could grow from a big toe.

TRAVELING BUTTERFLIES

Like some birds, Monarch butterflies go south in winter to get away from the cold. In summer they fly back north. It is a hard trip both ways. As they travel, many are killed. Mice, ants, and other insects and animals eat them. Storms tear their wings. But they keep on.

Every year, they make stops at the same places. There is a town in California known as Butterfly Town. Monarchs stop there on their way south. Until 1975, no one was sure where the Monarch butterflies spent the winter. They knew it was Mexico, but they didn't know quite where. Mexican woodcutters found them. On a mountain hill were a thousand trees covered with millions of butterflies.

Scientists can tell how far and where butterflies go. To do this, the scientists put tiny red tags on them. They get other people who are not scientists to do this, too. The tags give the place and time that the butterfly was caught. People who find tagged butterflies send them to a central place. There, scientists keep records of how far and fast butterflies travel. One butterfly flew 80 miles in one day.

The mystery? Monarch butterflies live about a year. The ones that fly north were born in the south. They have never seen the north before. How do they know where to go?

READING QUESTIONS

Choose the best answer. Write in your notebook the number of each question and the letter—a, b, c, or d—that shows the best answer.

1. What are the stories mostly about?

    (a) Unusual ways animals travel

   (b) Unusual things some animals do

   (c) The unusual strength of some animals

   (d) The unusual color that some animals have

2. What does one story suggest is a problem for lemmings?
   (a) Their eyesight
   (b) Wolves
   (c) Overpopulation
   (d) Disease

3. What is a sponge made of?
   (a) Small fish
   (b) Tiny animals
   (c) Large insects
   (d) Green plants

4. What happens if you break up a sponge and put it in a tank?
   (a) It makes lots of new sponges.
   (b) It turns into a fish.
   (c) It comes back together as it was.
   (d) It turns into a sponge of a different shape.

5. What happens if a piece of a sponge is put on a rock?
   (a) It makes four new sponges.
   (b) It makes a whole new sponge like the one it came from.
   (c) It crawls off the rock and into the sand.
   (d) It grows flowers and then dies.

6. How long do Monarch butterflies usually live?
   (a) A week
   (b) Two weeks
   (c) A year
   (d) Five years

7. What do scientists use to tell how far and how fast butterflies go?
   (a) The sun
   (b) Phone calls
   (c) Red tags
   (d) Radar

8. What was not known about Monarch butterflies until 1975?
   (a) That they travel long distances
   (b) That they spend the winter on a hill in Mexico
   (c) That they visit a town in California
   (d) That they are killed by mice and ants

WORDS TO KNOW

Choose the word that best fits the blank in each sentence.
Write it in your notebook beside the number of the sentence.

Monarch   sponge   lemming   scientists

1. A _____ is an animal like a rat with a short tail.

2. A _____ is made up of many little animals.

3. People who study nature are _____ .

4. _____ butterflies fly south in winter.

SPEAKING AND LISTENING

Discuss these questions with your classmates.
1. What is the idea some scientists have as to why lemmings start running? Do you think they are right? Can you think of another reason lemmings might run? What is it?

2.   Sponges are tiny animals that live together in a colony. What other animals live in colonies? How are they like the sponge? How are they different?

3.   We don't know how Monarch butterflies know where to travel. What do you think the answer is?

WAYS OF FINDING OUT

Scientists have different ways of finding things out. Most of the time, they pick a way that fits what they are looking for. For example, they might tag a deer to find out where it wanders.

Copy the following two columns on a piece of paper. Draw a line from each question to the way of finding out that matches it.

Question

What happens to a broken sponge?

Why do lemmings sometimes run to their deaths?

How far do butterflies go?

Way of Finding Out

Put tags on them.

Check the food supply.

Put the pieces in a tank.

STUDYING AN ANIMAL

Choose an animal or insect. You might pick your dog, a squirrel, a cockroach, an ant. Keep a record of everything it does for one hour. What did you find out?

READING, WRITING, AND SPEAKING ABOUT IT

Find and read an article about the habits or abilities of an animal. Make notes about what you read. Then, tell the class what you learned. Here are some examples of possible subjects.

1. Ways dolphins "talk" to each other
2. Birds that lay eggs in other birds' nests
3. Bird flyways in North America
4. Ways animals use tools

9

THE LOCH NESS MONSTER

PLACES

Loch Ness [LAHK NES] a long lake in Scotland, where a monster is said to live

Scotland [SKAHT-lund] a country in western Europe

PEOPLE

Alex Campbell [AL-iks KAM-bul] a man who lives in Scotland

Winifred Cary [WIN-uh-frid CAIR-ee] a woman who lives in Scotland

Tim Dinsdale [TIM DINZ-dayl] a photographer

WORDS

evidence [EV-uh-duhnz] an outward sign; something that gives proof

mast [MAST] a pole sticking straight up that holds a sail on a boat or ship

plesiosaur [PLEE-see-uh-sawr] a kind of reptile that is supposed to have died out long ago

snail [SNAYL] an animal that lives in a shell

sonar [SOH-nar] a machine for finding underwater objects by bouncing sound off them

Loch Ness is a narrow lake in Scotland. In some places, it is nearly 1,000 feet deep. Thousands of years ago, it was part of the ocean. Then an ice sheet pushed a ridge of rocks that slowly cut it off from the ocean. The lake never freezes. Its waters are dark. Once, it is said, some divers working in Loch Ness brushed against a huge thing at the bottom. They were so afraid their hair turned white. Maybe that huge thing was a monster. Some people think that a monster lives in Loch Ness.

In 1917, when she was eleven, Winifred Cary went fishing with her brother. They went out on Loch Ness in a boat. Then they saw what they thought was a monster. Winifred said later it was a huge thing. She said, "It was going fast against the wind. It was up only for a second or so. Of course, no one believed us when we told them."

When a road was built by the lake, more people traveled there. And more people said they saw a monster. Since then, the monster has been "seen" more than 3,000 times.

In 1933, a man and a woman said they saw a monster cross the road. It was like a huge snail five feet high. The next year, Alex Campbell said he saw it. Its neck was sticking up out of the water six feet. Then a boat came along. The monster dived under the water. Campbell says he has seen the monster 17 more times.

Winifred Cary said she saw a monster again in 1954. The lake was calm that day. She was standing on a hill feeding hens. Then she said she saw something on the far side of the loch. It was a mile and a half away. At first she thought it was a boat with a mast. But she couldn't understand why such a big boat would be so close to shore. The thing was 30 or 40 feet long. Then it turned and came rushing toward Winifred. It was going across the lake very fast. As it came nearer, she could see that it had no mast. What she had seen must have

The humps in the water are said to belong to the Loch Ness monster.

been a head and neck. A large fish jumped out of its way. The monster must have been chasing it. It had a huge hump, Winifred said.

In that same year, a group of people on a bus watched the monster for ten minutes. It was only 100 yards away. It has also been seen by a priest and two police officers.

What do people see when they see the monster? Humps in the water, like upturned boats in a line. A long neck with a head about the size of a horse's head. Something about 30 feet long and dark in color. The monster moves fast—about ten miles an hour. It is shy and hates noise.

The question is this: Is there a monster? There is some evidence. In 1934, a doctor took a picture of what looks like a monster's head and neck. In 1960, Tim Dinsdale, who had

Dr. Harlow E. Edgerton holds two photos he believes to be of the Loch Ness monster.

watched the lake for more than three days, saw a hump come up. It looked like a big log. Then it started to move. He took 40 feet of film of the monster moving to shore. The next day, Dinsdale made a film of a fast boat going over the same route. The first film seemed to show something going about ten miles an hour.

Since the 1960s, scientists have been trying to find out if there is a monster. They play sounds to bring it closer. They put out bait. Cameras are sent down. Sonar is used to check the lake for large things underwater. The sonar has found many things, but not the monster: a large flying boat, teapots, tires, and dozens of shoes. One scientist joked that he knew what the monster was. It was nothing, he said, but a huge shoe.

Some photographs from under the water show a fin shape. Another shows a head shape. And still another looks like a huge body. But the photographs don't show enough to prove anything.

If there is a monster, what is it? Some say it is a plesiosaur. The plesiosaurs lived when dinosaurs did—long ago. They should have died out. Is it possible that a few did not? If so, some questions need to be asked. How does the monster breathe? The plesiosaur lived in the ocean but breathed air. Does the monster come up for air? How often? How did the earlier plesiosaurs live through the time of the ice sheet? What happens to dead monsters? Not one has been found. And no bones have been found either.

READING QUESTIONS

Choose the best answer. Write in your notebook the number of each question and the letter—a, b, c, or d—that shows the best answer.

1. What is this story mostly about?

    (a) The size of some monsters

    (b) Damage caused by a monster

    (c) People who have seen a monster

    (d) Photographs taken of a monster

2. How was Loch Ness cut off from the ocean?

    (a) It dried up.

    (b) A ridge of rocks cut it off.

    (c) People built a dam.

    (d) No one knows.

3. How many times has the monster been seen?

   (a) More than 3,000 times

   (b) Less than 2,000 times

   (c) About 50 times

   (d) Only once

4. What did the monster look like when it crossed the road?

   (a) A plesiosaur

   (b) A huge snail

   (c) A huge worm

   (d) A seal

5. How long is the monster supposed to be?

   (a) About eight feet long

   (b) About 100 feet long

   (c) Ten feet long

   (d) About 30 feet long

6. What did one scientist joke that the monster might be?

   (a) A giant shoe

   (b) A sunken boat

   (c) A fallen tree

   (d) A huge rock

7. What might the monster really be?

   (a) A plesiosaur

   (b) A brontosaurus

   (c) A dragon

   (d) An elephant

8. Where did plesiosaurs live?

    (a) On land

    (b) In the ocean

    (c) In trees

    (d) In the mountains

WORDS TO KNOW

Choose the word that best fits the blank in each sentence. Write it in your notebook beside the number of the sentence.

plesiosaur mast sonar evidence snail

1. The sail was ripped off the _____ by a storm.

2. The _____ lived in the time of the dinosaurs.

3. With _____ , scientists have checked to see what objects lie at the bottom of the lake.

4. The monster looked like a huge _____ as it crossed the road.

5. The film of the monster gives _____ that perhaps there is a real monster.

SPEAKING AND LISTENING

Discuss these questions with your classmates.

1. What evidence is there that dinosaurs were real? What evidence is there that the Loch Ness monster is real? Are bones better evidence than stories from people who say they have seen a monster? Why?

2. Do you think the Loch Ness monster is real? Why?

3. What might the Loch Ness monster be? Why do you say so?

4. In what ways have scientists been trying to prove that the monster is real? What have they found? Why is the evidence not enough to prove anything?

5. How might a large number of people see something that isn't there?

THE SOURCE

Evidence given by some people is more likely to be true than evidence given by other people. For example, you might be more likely to believe evidence about the monster from a scientist than from a story writer. Using the numbers 1 through 11, rank these people as sources of evidence about the Loch Ness monster. The one you would believe most would get a number 1. Then tell why you ranked them as you did.

a. police officer   b. scientist   c. photographer

d. diver   e. fisherman   f. minister

g. politician   h. teacher   i. store owner

j. tourist   k. journalist

READING AND WRITING DETAILS

In the story, find sentences that answer these questions. Write those sentences on a piece of paper.

1. What caused Loch Ness to be separated from the ocean?

2. How many times since the road was built has the monster been seen?

3. How fast is the monster said to move?

4. What did Dinsdale do so experts could compare his monster film with something else?

5. How long have scientists been trying to prove whether or not there is a monster?

10

THE DISCOVERY OF THE GORILLA

PLACES

Africa [AF-ruh-kuh] a large piece of land containing many countries

Europe [YOO-rup] a large piece of land containing many countries

PEOPLE

Paul de Chaillu [PAWL duh CHIE-loo] an explorer from the United States

Doctor Savage [DOK-ter SAV-uj] the first American to see a gorilla

WORDS

explorer [iks-PLOR-er] a person who finds out about unknown places

gorilla [guh-RIL-uh] a kind of large ape

knuckles [NUK-ulz] places where the fingers bend

skull [SKUL] the bones of the head

travelers [TRAV-uh-lerz] people who go from place to place

Europe and Africa are two separate places. They are quite far apart. For a long time, Europeans did not know very much about Africa. True, some parts of Africa were ruled by European countries. And European explorers had gone into places deep inside Africa. But most Europeans forgot one thing. They forgot that maybe Africans knew more about Africa than people from Europe could. That is why they didn't believe stories about a monster who turned out to be real.

It was more than a hundred years ago. Africans had told Europeans about a monster animal. This animal, they said, was a big ape. It was covered with hair. Though it was about as big as a man, it weighed more. When angry, it pounded its chest with its big fists. Its eyes glared from under its huge

brows. It was not a monster that a person would care to meet.

Some travelers from Europe said they had seen this monster. They called it a gorilla. But most Europeans thought the stories about the gorilla were just that—stories. They thought the Africans made up the gorilla to scare themselves. They thought it was not real. It was a monster that never was—like the dragon, they said.

In 1847, an American named Doctor Savage was in Africa. Someone showed him the skull of a huge monster. The Africans said the skull came from an animal called "engeena." Savage thought it was a gorilla skull. He decided there was a gorilla after all. He went out and found some more gorilla bones. Then he paid some Africans to kill two gorillas for him. That gave proof that the monster was real. The gorilla was "found." The Africans had known it was real all along.

Not long after that, an explorer named Paul de Chaillu came to Africa. He studied apes there. Some of the apes he studied were gorillas. In a book, de Chaillu told stories about gorillas. Gorillas were fierce, he said. They stole women and children and ate them, he said. People believed his stories. Seeing gorilla pictures made the stories easy to believe. The gorilla *looks* mean.

Europeans wanted to see a live gorilla. Pictures weren't enough. But they didn't want to go all the way to Africa to see one. So it was decided to send gorillas to Europe and put them in zoos. Explorers began catching gorillas. Then the gorillas were shut up in cages and put on ships. Most of the gorillas didn't make it as far as Europe. They died on the ships. The gorillas couldn't stand being shut up.

If gorillas were to talk, they would say that people are the monsters. Gorillas mind their own business. They like peace and quiet. They never eat people. In fact, meat is not their main food. Mostly they eat bark, leaves, roots, and fruit.

Sometimes they eat small animals and birds' eggs. Gorillas are very shy. That's why it took so long for Europeans to find them. If gorillas hear a noise, they hide out.

It is true that the gorilla can seem scary. It roars and beats its hands against its chest. That makes a deep, loud sound. Why does the gorilla do it? It's a bluff. It's done to scare people away. The gorilla will bite only if there's no other way out.

The gorilla's big brow over its eyes makes it look mean. Its arms are long and strong. It walks on its back legs and its knuckles.

Gorillas live simple lives in small groups. During the day they wander, looking for food. At night they make nests on the ground or in trees. They sleep in the nests.

The gorilla is a good example of the idea that looks are not always a mirror of the way an animal behaves. This creature that looks like a monster is really a gentle animal.

READING QUESTIONS

Choose the best answer. Write in your notebook the number of each question and the letter—a, b, c, or d—that shows the best answer.

1. What is this story mostly about?
   (a) What gorillas eat
   (b) How gorillas live
   (c) How gorillas were found
   (d) What gorillas look like

2. What did some people think about the gorilla stories at first?
   (a) That the stories were sad
   (b) That some people made the stories up
   (c) That the gorilla was shy
   (d) That gorillas were extinct

3. What was the first clue Doctor Savage had that the gorilla was a real animal?
   (a) Footprints
   (b) A photograph
   (c) A drawing
   (d) A skull

4. What proof did Savage get to show that the gorilla was real?
   (a) Stories
   (b) Two dead gorillas
   (c) A photograph
   (d) A book

5. Why did explorers catch gorillas?
   (a) To sell for food
   (b) To use in experiments
   (c) To put in zoos
   (d) To have as pets

6. How would gorillas view people if they could talk?
   (a) As helpful beings
   (b) As heartless and cruel
   (c) As a kind of food
   (d) As a type of bird

7. Why do gorillas beat their chests?
   (a) To show they are ready to kill
   (b) To scare people away
   (c) To get ready to fight
   (d) To show off for each other

8. Where do gorillas sleep?
   (a) On the bare ground
   (b) In huts
   (c) In caves
   (d) In nests they make

WORDS TO KNOW

Choose the word that best fits the blank in each sentence. Write it in your notebook beside the number of the sentence.

explorer   travelers   gorilla   skull   knuckles

1. The gorilla walks on its back legs and its _____ .

2. A person who finds out about unknown places is called an _____ .

3. A _____ is a gentle ape.

4. Among the other bones, they found a gorilla _____ .

5. The _____ decided to take a trip to Africa.

SPEAKING AND LISTENING

Discuss these questions with your classmates.

1. Why did some people think the gorilla was not real?

2. Do you think there are other animals that have not been found yet? Where might they be found, do you think?

3. What made people think the gorilla was fierce? What does this tell you about evidence?

4. Was it fair to cage the gorillas on a ship? Why?

5. Is it fair to keep animals in zoos? Why?

FINDING IT

Find Europe and Africa on a map or globe. How far apart are they? How can you get from one to the other? Before there were airplanes, what was probably the best way? Why?

LANGUAGE

The Africans had their own word for "gorilla." It was "enge-ena." Write words in other languages that you know. Next to each word, write the English word that means the same thing.

WRITING A COMPARISON

Watch an animal for one hour to see what it does. Write down how it behaves. What does it do when it meets another animal? Does it bluff? How? Does it show it is friendly? How? Now watch a person for an hour to see what he or she does. What does the person do when he or she meets another person? Does the person do any bluffing? How does he or she act friendly? Write a few sentences comparing the animal and the person.

11

STRANGE ANIMALS

PLACES

Australia [aws-TRAYL-yuh] a large piece of land in the Pacific

Colorado Rocky Mountains [kah-luh-RAH-doh RAHK-ee MOWN-tuhnz] mountains in the state of Colorado in the western United States

WORDS

angler fish [ANG-ler FISH] ocean fish

batteries [BAT-er-eez] cells that give electric power

bower [BOW-er] a place to get under cover

bowerbird [BOW-er-berd] an Australian bird that builds things
electric eel [ee-LEK-trik EEL] a fish that can give a shock
female [FEE-mayl] an animal of the sex that can bear children
male [MAYL] an animal of the sex that can father children
water ouzel [WAH-ter OOZ-ul] a small brown songbird

The world is full of strange animals. Some are so strange you might wonder how they came to be. You might think that someone made them up. These four are like that. But, believe it or not, they are real. They are as real as people, who can be very strange, too.

THE ELECTRIC EEL

The electric eel comes from South America. One that is full-grown can kill a person. In a way, the eel has a death ray. The death ray is an electric shock. The bigger the eel, the bigger the shock. The shock a baby eel gives off is weak. A little tickle, maybe. But the shock from a nine-foot eel is another story. A big eel can even hurt itself. If you put a big eel in salt water, it can kill itself with its own death ray.

The power from an electric eel can light a sign. Once, the power from an eel was used to light a sign that said "Electric Eel." Another time, eel power started up the engine

The head of an electric eel.

on a fireboat. How does the electric eel work up a shock? Three-fourths of an electric eel's body is made up of tiny cells like batteries. Each cell makes a small amount of electric power. The eel can switch the cells on and off. When it switches them on, it gives off a shock. All the cells send out power at once. The eel does this to kill food. If you are in the way, watch out!

THE WATER OUZEL

The water ouzel is a small brown bird. It lives in the Colorado Rocky Mountains. It is not much to look at. But it can do strange things. Perhaps the strangest thing it does is fly under the water. Along the bottom it goes. Its wings are flapping. It holds onto stones there with its sharp claws. It pecks away among those stones eating bugs. Then it comes up to breathe and dry off.

The water ouzel lives behind a waterfall. In back of the wall of falling water, there is a dry place. The water ouzel is safe there. On the rocks it builds a moss nest. Water ouzels can sing. But the sound of the falls is too loud for them to hear. So they talk to each other by flashing their white eyelids.

THE ANGLER FISH

The angler fish has a built-in fishing pole. From its back, there grows a kind of rod. From the rod, a "line" comes down in

front of the angler fish's nose. On the end of the "line," there is something that looks like a tasty worm. On some angler fish, the "worm" glows in the dark. The whole thing—"rod," "line," and "worm"—is really part of the angler fish's body.

The angler fish lives on the sea bottom. Sometimes it is partly hidden in the sand. The rod waves the line back and forth. Soon a little fish will see the "worm." It will come over to eat the "worm." When it does, the angler fish opens its big mouth and snaps up the little fish.

THE BOWERBIRD

Many bowerbirds live in Australia. The male bowerbirds go to a lot of trouble to please the females. They build fancy bowers. But the bowers are not nests. They are just to interest the females. One kind of bowerbird builds a walled path. It takes sticks in its beak. Then it drives the sticks into the ground to build walls. The walls are about four inches apart. The bowerbird holds them up by winding vines in them. Then the bird covers the floor of the walled path with different things: flowers and shells, white bones, pieces of broken dishes, rags, colored stones. The bowerbird loves the color blue. Sometimes it steals blue things from people. One bird stole some blue clothespins. The bird makes up paint from spit, berry juice, and dirt. He paints the walls of his bower. To do this, he uses a twig or a leaf as a brush. All of the building is to catch a female's eye. When a female comes around, the male sometimes holds a flower in his beak. He dances around her. He shows her the walled path. If he is lucky, he becomes her mate.

READING QUESTIONS

Choose the best answer. Write in your notebook the number of each question and the letter—a, b, c, or d—that shows the best answer.

1. What are these stories mostly about?
   (a) The ways animals get food
   (b) The odd things some animals do
   (c) The way some animals look
   (d) The hard life some animals live

2. Where does the shock from an electric eel come from?
   (a) From tiny cells like batteries
   (b) From its tongue
   (c) From an electric outlet
   (d) From its feet

3. How much of an eel's body is made up of cells like batteries?
   (a) One-fourth
   (b) One-half
   (c) Three-fourths
   (d) All of it

4. Where do water ouzels nest?
   (a) Behind waterfalls

  (b) In the rocks
  (c) Under water
  (d) In trees

5. How do water ouzels talk to each other?
  (a) By singing
  (b) By flashing their white eyelids
  (c) By flapping their wings
  (d) By pecking with their beaks

6. How does the angler fish bring little fish to itself?
  (a) With a noise
  (b) With sonar
  (c) With a fake "worm"
  (d) With its eyes

7. Why do male bowerbirds build bowers?
  (a) To make nests
  (b) To have fun
  (c) To produce art
  (d) To please female bowerbirds

8. What does the bowerbird use to paint the walls?
  (a) A brush
  (b) A twig or leaf
  (c) Its beak
  (d) Its wing

WORDS TO KNOW

Choose the word that best fits the blank in each sentence.
Write it in your notebook beside the number of the sentence.

> **batteries   male   female   water ouzel   bower
> bowerbird   angler fish   electric eel**

1. To get out of the rain, they ran into the _____.

2. A _____ lives behind a waterfall.

3. The cells in the body of an electric eel are like tiny _____ .

4. The _____ has a built-in fishing pole.

5. The _____ lives in Australia.

6. A full-grown _____ can kill a person with a shock.

7. A _____ can bear children.

8. A _____ can father children.

SPEAKING AND LISTENING

Discuss these questions with your classmates.

1. The electric eel catches its food with an electric shock. Do you know of other animals that get their food in unusual ways?

2. What other animal has a part that lights up?

3. Why does the water ouzel live behind a waterfall? Why can't its enemies get at it there? What other places do animals live in to be safe?

4. The angler fish has a part that looks like something else. Do you know of another animal that has a part that looks like something else? What is it? How does the part work?

5. The male bowerbird goes to a lot of trouble to please the female. What does it do? How do ther animals attract their mates?

FINDING IT

On a map or globe, find Australia. Notice that it is not attached to other land. What do you know about Australia's animals? How are they different from animals in other places? Why might this be?

CLASSIFYING

Both the bowerbird and the water ouzel belong to the class called *birds*. So do robins and sparrows.

Copy the following four classes of things on a piece of paper. Then read the list of items below. On your paper, write each item under the class to which it belongs.

Classes: vegetables   things to drink   fish   tools

Items:

paintbrush   potato   tea

angler fish   pen   comb

electric eel   water   carrot

orange juice   peas

WRITING ABOUT SCIENCE

In an encyclopedia or book about animals, find the answers to these questions. Write the answers on a separate piece of paper.

1. Why is salt water a danger for an electric eel? How does the salt water make the electric eel shock itself?

2. Why does the bowerbird like the color blue?

12

THE ALMAS OF THE SOVIET UNION

PLACE

Soviet Union [SOH-vee-et YOON-yun] a large country in Europe and Asia

PEOPLE AND CREATURES

Almas [AHL-mus] a creature that looks something like an ape and something like a human

A. Khakhlov [KAHK-luv] a Russian scientist

Jeanne Kofman [JEEN KAWF-mun] a Russian doctor

A. G. Pronin [PROH-neen] a Russian scientist
Russians [RUSH-unz] people who live in the Soviet Union
Zana [ZAH-nuh] an Almas

WORDS

insects [IN-sektz] small animals of the group containing bugs and
   bees
reports [ree-PORTZ] facts put together to make up true stories
thief [THEEF] someone who steals

101

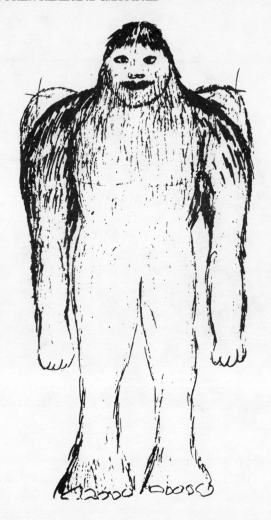

Stories about ape-men have been told in many places. In the United States, such a creature is called Bigfoot. In the Soviet Union, its name is Almas. The Russians have been looking for a live Almas for years. Jeanne Kofman, a doctor, is one of the researchers. She has gotten more than 300 reports from people who say they have seen an Almas. Or they say they have seen some Almas footprints about 12 inches long. The reports agree on what an Almas looks like. Its forehead is low. Its cheekbones are high. Its nose is small and flat. It doesn't have much of a chin. Here are four stories about Almas. The first is from more than a hundred years ago.

ZANA

Back about a hundred years ago, hunters caught an Almas. She looked like an ape-woman. All over her body was thick black hair. When the hunters tried to tie her up, she fought them. So they hit her with clubs. Then they put a gag in her mouth and tied her legs to a log.

People called her Zana. First she belonged to a prince. Then she was taken to a small village. There her keeper put her inside a strong fence, where she lived like a wild animal. The keeper threw her food at her. She dug a hole in the ground to sleep in. For three years, she lived this way. Then, because she was tamer, her keeper brought her closer to the house. At first she was tied, but at last she was set free. She did not leave.

Zana worked for her keeper. When he told her to, she carried wood or ground the grain. She never learned to speak. But she did make sounds. When her keeper shouted at her, she was afraid. Yet she was strong enough to be able to beat him up. With her big teeth she could crack anything. She could run faster than a horse. Even when the river was high, she could swim it. Zana loved grapes. She pulled down vines to eat them. She liked wine, too. Sometimes she got drunk on it.

The village children teased her with sticks. When they did, she grabbed the sticks and broke them. She chased the children away. But she never hurt them.

They say Zana is buried in the village. She died there nearly a hundred years ago. But scientists have not been able to find her bones.

TWO STORIES FOUND BY A. KHAKHLOV

In 1907, a scientist named A. Khakhlov started studying Almas. He went about finding stories from people who had seen them. Here are two of the stories he was told.

Two men were traveling through the mountains. At night, they put their horses out to eat grass. When the sun came up, a creature was near the horses. The men thought it was a horse thief. So they chased it on their horses. The creature ran slowly, so they were able to rope it. It squeaked like a rabbit. It was a male Almas. The Almas was covered with hair. His arms were long. He had a big brow and not much chin. He walked with legs apart, bent at the knees. He feet were broader than a man's. The big toe was set apart from the others. One of the men said an Almas would never hurt people, so they should set him free. They did. Then they followed him. The Almas lived in a spot under a cliff. He had made a kind of grass nest there.

A female Almas was caught by farmers. She looked like the male Almas the men in Khakhlov's first story found. When angry, she bared her teeth. She slept with her knees and elbows under her. The food she ate was raw meat, greens, and grain. Later, she decided she liked bread better than meat. If insects came close, she ate them. She had two ways of drinking water. Sometimes she lay down and put her face in the water to drink. Other times she dripped the water into her mouth with her hand. In the end the farmers set her free. She ran away and hid.

A. G. PRONIN'S STORY

In 1959, A. G. Pronin, a Russian scientist, was high in the mountains. He and some others were going to do some work there. The rest of the group had gone with the horses into a town. Pronin was left alone. At noon one day, he walked up the valley. On a hill about 500 yards away, he saw a strange creature. It looked like a man, but it was not a man. Its arms were very long. It was standing against the snow. All Pronin could see clearly was its shape. Its legs were wide apart. For five minutes Pronin watched it. Then it went behind a rock. Three days later, after sunset, Pronin saw the creature again. It stood at the same place. Then it went into what looked like a cave. Pronin wanted to get closer to it. He couldn't. The mountain in that place was too steep to climb. A week later, the rest of the group came. Their work was noisy. No creatures were seen. Just before the group left, they found that their boat was missing. They looked for it, but they couldn't find it. A month later, other scientists found the boat miles upstream. It

was in good shape. How did it get there? The river ran fast the other way. The people from the village said that Almas sometimes stole things. Then they left what they stole in the mountains. Had the creature or others like it taken the boat?

READING QUESTIONS

Choose the best answer. Write in your notebook the number of each question and the letter—a, b, c, or d—that shows the best answer.

1. What are these stories mostly about?
   (a) Farmers who have seen big creatures
   (b) Several big creatures that have been seen in the Soviet Union
   (c) The difficulty of taking care of big creatures
   (d) A scientist who captured two big creatures

2. Where did Zana live after she was first caught?
   (a) In a cave
   (b) Inside a fence
   (c) In a house
   (d) In a tree

3. Where did Zana sleep?
   (a) In a room
   (b) In a tree
   (c) In a hole in the ground
   (d) In a nest

4. What did Zana do when children teased her?
   (a) She broke the sticks and chased the children.
   (b) She killed all the children she could catch.
   (c) She acted as though the children were not there.
   (d) She called the police.

5. Where is Zana supposed to be now?
   (a) In the forest
   (b) In a room

    (c) On a ship

    (d) In a grave in the village

6. What sound did the Almas in the first of Khakhlov's stories make?

    (a) A roar

    (b) A sound like a rabbit

    (c) A crying noise

    (d) A scream

7. When did A. G. Pronin see an Almas?

    (a) A hundred years ago

    (b) In 1907

    (c) In 1977

    (d) In 1959

8. Why didn't Pronin try to get closer to the Almas?

    (a) It was too far away.

    (b) The mountain there was too steep.

    (c) The village people said not to.

    (d) He was afraid.

WORDS TO KNOW

Choose the word that best fits the blank in each sentence. Write it in your notebook beside the number of the sentence.

reports   thief   insects

1. The female Almas like to eat _____.

2. Jeanne Kofman had many _____ about Almas.

3. Someone who steals is a _____ .

SPEAKING AND LISTENING

Discuss these questions with your classmates.

1. What evidence is there that the Almas is real? How good is this evidence? What might lead you to believe the Almas is not real?

2. How did the people who caught Almas treat them? Was this right? Was it right to make Zana work without paying her? Was it right to fence her in? Why?

3. How might Zana have felt when she was teased?

4. How must she have felt about being taken from her home?

5. Why, do you think, didn't she beat up her keeper?

FINDING IT

Find the Soviet Union on a map. How big is it? Almas live in the mountains. Where are the mountains in the Soviet Union?

SHOWING IT

Look outside of the window. Figure out how far away 500 yards is. Now, if possible, look at a person from that distance. How much detail can you see? What does this tell you about Pronin's story?

WRITING A STORY

Write a story from Zana's point of view. Think of how the village must have looked to her. Think of what must have surprised her. Remember, the Almas live simple lives. They know nothing of houses and other human things.

RANKING THE STORIES

Reread the stories told in this section. Decide which is the easiest to believe. Write the title of that story at the top of a piece of paper. Put a 1 next to it. Then, decide which story is the next easiest one to believe. Put a 2 next to it. Decide which story is the least easy to believe. Put a 3 next to it. (You may count Khakhlov's stories as one story.) Why have you ranked the stories this way? What part did time play? How much did you think about *who* was telling the story?

COMPARING

Copy the following chart on a piece of paper. Using the chart, compare the Almas in the four stories. Write in the blank spaces. If there is nothing to write, draw a line.

| | Zana | Pronin's Almas | Khakhlov's stories | |
			First Alma	Second Alma
Hair				
Where it slept				
What it ate				
Sounds it made				
Arms				
Brow				
Chin				
Way of walking				
Feet				
How it slept				
How it drank				

OUTLINING

Copy this outline on a separate piece of paper. Then fill in the blanks. Use the information in the chart in this section, if you like.

Almas

  A. How an Almas Is Like a Human Being

    1. _____

    2. _____

  B. How an Almas Is Like an Ape

    1. _____

    2. _____

    3. _____

unit
3

ADVENTURES INTO the UNKNOWN

13

FOUR MYSTERIES

PLACES

Egypt [EE-jipt] a country in northern Africa
France [FRANS] a country in western Europe
Greece [GREES] a country in southern Europe
Peru [puh-ROO] a country in South America

PEOPLE AND THINGS

Nazca [NAZ-kuh] a group of people who lived in Peru
Cheops [KEE-ops] an Egyptian king

WORDS

ceramics [suh-RAM-iks] things made of baked clay

dowsing [DOW-zing] hunting for things under the ground

dunes [DOONZ] hills of sand in the desert

pyramid [PEER-uh-mid] an object with triangular sides that meet at the top

textiles [TEKS-tiels] woven cloths

Here are some short mysteries from all over the world. Why have they puzzled people for so long?

THE NAZCA LINES

In Peru there are strange paths that wind across the land. These paths seem to go nowhere. They are miles long. When seen from an airplane, these paths look like lines. Some of the lines make up drawings. These drawings are of spiders, birds, snakes, fish, and flowers. Some of these drawings are over 30 miles long. They are found in a place called the Red Plain. Here if you pick up the red brown stones, you can see the light soil. Pick up a row of rocks and you see a line. That is how the drawings were made.

These drawings were made over 1,000 years ago. At that time a culture called the Nazca lived in Peru. These people were skilled in art. They made beautiful ceramics and elaborate textiles. The huge drawings are called the Nazca Lines.

When the Nazca Lines were made, there were no large machines. The lines had to be made by hand. There were no airplanes. No one could see what the finished drawings looked like.

The Question: Why did people make the huge drawings?

THE CHEOPS PYRAMID

The Cheops Pyramid was built about 4,500 years ago. It stands 40 stories high. In it are 2,500,000 stones. Many of those stones weigh 2 1/2 tons, as much as 2 1/2 small cars each. You can't get a piece of paper between those stones. If you laid them out, you could build a wall one stone high around France. The Pyramid was built by the Egyptians—more than 100,000 of them. They worked three months a year for 22 years on it.

The Questions: How did the Egyptians carry the stones? How was the Pyramid built?

SINGING DUNES

Some sand dunes make strange noises. They sing, scream, bark, and boom. One place they are being studied is the Devil's Playground in California. Singing sand dunes have a certain shape. One side is steep and the other side is long and rises slowly. The shape of the dunes may cause the wind to make noises around them.

The Question: Why do the sand dunes sing?

DOWSING RODS

Some people say they can find water and metal under the ground by using dowsing rods. People have tried this for more than 600 years. The people who do this are called dowsers. The rods they use are made of a twig shaped like a *Y* or from two *L*-shaped pieces of wire. Dowsers pick up the forked ends of the stick or ends of the wire. Then they walk across the ground. When the rod is over metal or water, the rod is supposed to pull down. Some people say the rods can find water or metal hundreds of feet deep in the earth. In a war a few years ago, some people used wire dowsing rods to try to find land mines.

The Question: Do dowsing rods really work?

READING QUESTIONS

Choose the best answer. Write in your notebook the number of each question and the letter—a, b, c, or d—that shows the best answer.

1. What are these stories mostly about?
   (a) Unusual people
   (b) Large buildings
   (c) Unsolved mysteries
   (d) Strange animals

2. What do the Nazca Lines show?
   (a) Words in an old language
   (b) The walls of buildings
   (c) Animals, flowers, and birds
   (d) Triangles, squares, and circles only

3. Where are the Nazca Lines?
   (a) In Mexico
   (b) In Peru
   (c) In Brazil
   (d) In Ecuador

4. When was the Cheops Pyramid built?
   (a) 700 years ago
   (b) 2,000 years ago
   (c) 4,500 years ago
   (d) 8,200 years ago

5. How many months altogether did people work to build the Cheops Pyramid?
   (a) 3
   (b) 22
   (c) 66
   (d) 88

6. What is special about singing dunes?
   (a) How hot they are
   (b) How they are shaped
   (c) How small they are
   (d) How they move

7. What are dowsing rods used for?
   (a) To find missing people
   (b) To find metals and water
   (c) To make magic rings
   (d) To do arithmetic

8. How are dowsers supposed to know when they have found what they are looking for?
   (a) The rod shocks them.
   (b) The rod makes a noise.
   (c) The rod pulls down.
   (d) The rod shakes out of their hands.

WORDS TO KNOW

Choose the word that best fits the blank in each sentence. Write it in your notebook beside the number of the sentence.

ceramics   dunes   dowsing   textiles   pyramid

1. A _____ has three sides that meet at the top.

2. In the desert, sand piles up and makes _____.

3. In Peru, they wove beautiful _____.

4. The hardened _____ came out of the bake oven.

5. A _____ rod is a thing people use to try to find buried metal or water.

SPEAKING AND LISTENING

Discuss these questions with your classmates.

1. Here are some people's ideas about why the Nazca Lines were made. Pick the one you think is best. Why do you think so?
   (a) As a form of art
   (b) To act as a "desert calendar"
   (c) To say something to the gods
   (d) To show that people from outer space have been to Earth

2. Here are some ideas about why the sand dunes sing. Which do you like best? Why?
   (a) The wind whistles around them because of their shape.
   (b) Little animals inside the dunes make whistling noises.
   (c) The sand blows in people's ears and they think they hear singing.

3. Here are some ideas people have about dowsing rods. Which do you find most likely? Why?
   (a) The dowser has a feeling where the water or metal is. The dowser moves the rod because of the feeling.
   (b) Water and metal give off waves that cause the rods to move.
   (c) Dowsing rods don't work at all. If they point to water or metal, it is because of a lucky guess on the part of the dowser.

FINDING IT

Look at an atlas or book of maps. Find Peru on a map of South America. Find Egypt on a map of Africa. Find California on a map of the United States. Copy the following two columns on a piece of paper. Draw a line from each place to what is there.

Place	What Is There
California	Where the Nazca Lines are
Peru	Where the Cheops Pyramid is
Egypt	Where some singing dunes are

DETAILS

In the stories, find sentences that answer these questions. Write those sentences on a piece of paper.
   1. How long are the Nazca Lines?
   2. Who built the Cheops Pyramid?
   3. What noises do singing dunes make?

4.   What are dowsing rods made of?

TIME LINE

2500		1	1000 1300	PRESENT
B.C.		A.D.	A.D. A.D	

Copy this time line on a piece of paper. Now write the following items on the time line, according to when they happened.

> Dowsing rods first used
> Cheops Pyramid built
> Nazca Lines made
> Singing sand dunes being studied

PROVING IT

Copy this chart on a piece of paper.

A *What Can't Be Proved*	B *What Can Be Proved*	C *How It Can Be Proved*

Now put the following phrases in column **A** or **B**. Then fill in column **C** for each item in column **B**.

> Why people made the Nazca Lines
> How much the Cheops Pyramid weighs
> How the Egyptians carried stones for pyramids
> What makes sand dunes sing
> That dowsing rods really work

14

WHO WAS KASPAR HAUSER?

PLACE

Germany [JERM-un-ee] a country in western Europe

PERSON

Kaspar Hauser [KAS-pur HOWZ-ur] a boy of seventeen

WORDS

liver [LIV-ur] a part of the body
swollen [SWOHL-un] grown bigger

The year was 1828 and the place a city in Germany when a tired boy of about seventeen stood on a doorstep.

The shoemaker opened the door. He saw the boy standing there. "Who are you?" he asked.

"I want to be a soldier as my father was," the boy said. The answer was odd. But the sentence the boy spoke was all he could say. He knew no other German.

His feet were swollen as if he had walked a long way. Or maybe he wasn't used to walking. His eyes were slitted up against the light. The shoemaker took the boy inside and

gave him food. Of all that was put before him, the boy ate only bread and water.

The shoemaker didn't know what else to do, so he took the boy to the police station. Perhaps the boy was lost. At the station the boy wrote his name on a piece of paper—Kaspar Hauser. He gave the police two letters. One said that Kaspar had been left with a stranger when he was very young. The other was from Kaspar's mother. She said she had been too poor to keep him.

For a while after Kaspar arrived, a teacher took care of him. He taught the boy German. At last Kaspar was able to tell about himself. He said he had been kept in a cell. The cell was only as long as a person is tall. It was four feet wide and five feet high. The floor was dirt. Kaspar had slept on straw. He had eaten only bread and water. His only toy was a small wooden horse. And that was all he remembered of his life.

There were strange things about Kaspar. He could not tell how far away something was by looking at it. He could see stars in the daytime. Noise and light bothered him. Often he sat looking off into space. The sound of a clock striking scared him. He was afraid of storms and moonlight, too. But he loved snow. Once he put his finger in a candle flame. When it burned him, he seemed surprised. Kaspar did not know what money was. He could not name colors very well. And to him, all people were "boy," and all animals were "horse."

After a while, a man from England took Kaspar. He had the idea in his head that Kaspar was the son of a king. He wanted to find out if he was right.

Now something else strange started to happen. It became clear that people were after Kaspar. Once a person whose face was painted black attacked Kaspar in a cellar. Why would anyone want to kill Kaspar? But someone did. In 1833, Kaspar went for a walk in a park with a person he did not know. It

A photo from a movie about Kaspar Hauser shows Kaspar holding his only toy—a wooden horse.

was a mistake. He was found in the snow—stabbed. There were no footprints in the snow but his. The knife was gone. Kaspar lived for three days. "I didn't do it myself," he said. "Many cats are the sure death of a mouse."

People who examined Kaspar's body after he was dead found that his liver was big. His legs were not straight. Both these facts would back up his story that he had lived in a small cell.

Who was he? Why did someone want to kill him? Was he a king's son? Which king? Did evil people keep him in the cell so someone else could rule a country? No one knows the answer. Chances are no one ever will.

READING QUESTIONS

Choose the best answer. Write in your notebook the number of each question and the letter—a, b, c, or d—that shows the best answer.

1. Which of the following titles best fits the story?
   (a) How Kaspar Hauser Learned to Talk
   (b) The Strange Case of Kaspar Hauser
   (c) What Kaspar Hauser Saw
   (d) Where Is Kaspar Hauser?

2. About how long ago did Kaspar Hauser live?
   (a) 10 years ago
   (b) 50 years ago
   (c) 150 years ago
   (d) 2,000 years ago

3. What did Kaspar say when the shoemaker asked who he was?
   (a) "I am Kaspar Hauser."
   (b) "Many cats are the sure death of a mouse."
   (c) "The moon shines in the west."

(d) "I want to be a soldier as my father was."

4. Why did Kaspar's mother say she had given him up?
   (a) She didn't like him.
   (b) Her husband told her to.
   (c) She was a queen.
   (d) She was too poor to keep him.

5. What was Kaspar afraid of?
   (a) People
   (b) Snow
   (c) Candle flames
   (d) Moonlight

6. Who did the man from England think Kaspar was?
   (a) The son of a king
   (b) An evil person
   (c) Someone from outer space
   (d) A poor boy

7. Who attacked Kaspar in the cellar?
   (a) The man from England
   (b) A person whose face was painted black
   (c) The teacher
   (d) His long-lost father

8. How did Kaspar die?
   (a) He got old.
   (b) He was stabbed.
   (c) He was shot.
   (d) His liver gave out.

WORDS TO KNOW

Choose the word that best fits the blank in each sentence. Write it in your notebook beside the number of the sentence.

bothered   swollen   liver

1. When you walk a long way, your feet might get _____.
2. Noise _____ Kaspar.
3. The _____ is inside a person's body.

CLASSIFICATION

When Kaspar called all people "boy," he was wrong about some of them. Some were girls. Some were men and women. Girls, boys, men, and women all are people. *People* is the big class in which we put them. Not all animals are horses. Some animals are cats, and some are dogs, lions, and turtles. The big class in which dogs, cats, lions, and turtles all fit is *animals*.

Copy the following four classes of things on a piece of paper. Then read the list of items below. On your paper, write each item under the class to which it belongs.

Classes:	people	machines	animals	food
Items:	milk	butterfly	duck	
	alligator	pizza	hot dogs	
	mother	butter	telephone	
	truck	toaster	sister	
	shoemaker	frog	teacher	
	radio	carrots	cow	
	firefighter	bicycle		

FINDING DETAILS

In the story, find sentences that answer these questions. Write those sentences on a piece of paper.

1. What told the shoemaker that Kaspar might have walked a long way?
2. Who was the first person to care for Kaspar?
3. What had Kaspar slept on in the cell?

4. What happened when Kaspar put his finger in the candle flame?

5. How was Kaspar killed?

SPEAKING AND LISTENING

Discuss these questions with your classmates.
1. Why might a person be locked up in a cell for life?

2. What facts in the story tell that Kaspar probably was locked up in a cell?

3. Why would light bother him? Why would noise?

4. What did Kaspar know? What did he not know?

PROVERBS

When Kaspar was about to die, he said, "Many cats are the sure death of a mouse." What did he mean by that? Explain the meanings of these other sayings.
1. Divide and rule.

2. Live today, for tomorrow we die.

3. It's a lot worse to be soul-hungry than to be body-hungry.

4. An eye for an eye, a tooth for a tooth.

5. Every dog has his day.

ASKING "WHAT IS TRUE?"

Discuss this question in class: Who was Kaspar Hauser? Then discuss these questions: Can any answer be proved? Why or why not?

15

ZIMBABWE – CITY OF AFRICA

PLACE

Zimbabwe [zim-BAB-wee] an old city in Africa

PEOPLE

Mutota [moo-TOH-tuh] king of Zimbabwe

Nguni [nih-GOO-nee] people from an African tribe

Karl Mauch [KARL MAWCH] a man who studied rocks

Willi Posselt [WEE-lee POH-zelt] an explorer

WORDS

ivory [EYE-vuh-ree] the thing elephant tusks are made of

ritual [RIT-yoo-ul] a form or way of acting used for certain things; for example, shaking hands

ruins [ROO-inz] a place that has been left and has fallen down, at least in part

tower [TOW-er] a building that is high and thin

Zimbabwe is a city in Africa that lived and died. Mystery has clung to it. Who built it? When? What for? We know some answers now, but not all.

Zimbabwe was a village for 2,500 years. Its people built round huts. And the shape of the village was also round. These people liked circles better than shapes with corners.

About 500 years ago, Zimbabwe was the center of a kingdom. It ruled a large part of southwestern Africa. The first king was Mutota. Gold and rare stones made him and those who came after him rich and powerful. The gold and rare stones came from the kingdom's mines. There was ivory from elephants. All these riches were taken through the forests to the sea. From there, boats took them to towns, where they were sold.

Around Zimbabwe was a wall of stone, which still stands. This wall is 32 feet high in some places. If you think about it, that's as high as a three-story building. No space shows between the stones in the wall. Nothing was used to hold them in place. They weigh a total of 15,000 tons. If you looked at the wall from the sky, it would be in the shape of a racetrack—no corners.

Inside the wall, the kings of Zimbabwe built a tower that looks like an upside-down cone. It, too, was made of stone.

Above it, in the rock, is another building. Near the building is a cave. A person talking in the cave can be heard in the tower. When the kings ruled, the place buzzed with people. Inside it were houses, places to hold grain, and other buildings.

Then in the 1700s, the kings of Zimbabwe lost a war with the Nguni tribe. The city fell into ruins. Bushes and thorn trees grew up in it. In a hundred years, it looked as though no one had lived there for a long time.

It was 1871 before people from Europe found Zimbabwe again. The first was Karl Mauch, a man who studied rocks. He had a feeling there was a city. So he asked where the nearest ruins were. The Africans told him. On the way there, he was captured by other Africans. But they let him go. And he found Zimbabwe. He said it was a valley filled with "houses of stone."

Not long after that, an explorer named Willi Posselt came to Zimbabwe. He told of how he and the people with him climbed on the wall. They walked along it to the tower. Then they grabbed vines. They used the vines to lower themselves into the ruins. It was very quiet. The people with him sat down and clapped their hands. It was a ritual. They knew about the old Zimbabwe, when kings ruled.

We still don't know what the tower was for. Some think it was built by a king to hold his gold. Others think it was built as a kind of church. And why, if you're in the tower, can you hear someone talking in the cave?

READING QUESTIONS

Choose the best answer. Write in your notebook the number of each question and the letter—a, b, c, or d—that shows the best answer.

1. What is this story mostly about?
   (a) How people built houses in Africa

(b) A city in Africa that lived and died

(c) A famous explorer of Africa

(d) The kings who ruled an African city

2. How high are the walls of Zimbabwe?

(a) 62 inches

(b) 32 feet

(c) 10 feet

(d) 800 feet

3. What does the tower look like?

(a) A cave

(b) An egg

(c) An African town

(d) An upside-down cone

4. How is the wall around Zimbabwe made?

(a) With stone and cement

(b) With stone cut to fit closely

(c) With stone and wood

(d) With stone and glass

5. What made Zimbabwe rich?

(a) Gold, rare stones, and ivory

(b) Oil and fish

(c) Trade with the the Nguni tribes

(d) Money from Europe

6. What happened to Zimbabwe?

(a) People from Europe took it.

(b) The kings died out.

(c) The gold mines gave out.

(d) It was conquered by the Nguni tribe.

7. Who was the first person from Europe to find Zimbabwe after it fell into ruins?

(a) King Mutota

(b) Willi Posselt

    (c) Karl Mauch
    (d) Tony Nguni

8. In what shape are African towns built?
    (a) A rough circle
    (b) A square
    (c) A diamond
    (d) A cone

WORDS TO KNOW

Choose the word that best fits the blank in each sentence. Write it in your notebook beside the number of each sentence.

      ritual   **ivory**   **ruins**   **tower**

1. Zimbabwe now lies in _____ .

2. They sold _____ , which comes from elephant tusks.

3. A _____ is a ceremony or religious custom.

4. The _____ was shaped like a cone.

SPEAKING AND LISTENING

Discuss these questions with your classmates.

1. What do you think the tower was for?

2. Why might people from Europe want to visit Zimbabwe?

3. Why might a person talking in the cave be heard in the tower?

4. Why might the Nguni tribe have gone to war with the kings of Zimbabwe?

5. What does the shape of the wall tell you about the people who built it?

WHEN SOMETHING IS LIKE SOMETHING ELSE

The story tells you the tower was shaped like an upside-down cone. The sentence used a cone, which you know about, to tell you something about the tower. Both the cone and the tower have the same shape. So they are alike in at least one way.

Write the following sentences on a piece of paper. Then fill in the blanks with the best answers.

1. The wall is shaped like _____.
    (a) a person
    (b) a racetrack
    (c) Africa
    (d) a cone

2. The wall is as high as _____.
    (a) a three-story building
    (b) gold
    (c) an egg
    (d) stone

3. The explorers used the vines as _____ to lower themselves.
    (a) leaves
    (b) food
    (c) ropes
    (d) money

4. The gold shone like _____.
    (a) books
    (b) the sun
    (c) the king
    (d) time

5. Each stone was as heavy as _____.
    (a) a car
    (b) ivory
    (c) air
    (d) the sun

FINDING IT

On a map of Africa, find Rhodesia. The ruins of Zimbabwe are in the southern part of Rhodesia.

RITUALS

When the Africans saw the ruins, they sat down and clapped their hands. This was a kind of ritual. What rituals do you have? Hint: What do you do when you say hello to someone?

16

TREASURE ON OAK ISLAND

PLACES

> **Oak Island** [OHK EYE-lund] an island off Nova Scotia
>
> **Nova Scotia** [NOH-vuh SKOH-shuh] a province in eastern Canada

WORDS

> **camera** [KAM-ruh] a thing that takes pictures
>
> **lumberjacks** [LUM-bur-jaks] people who cut down trees for a living
>
> **machine** [muh-SHEEN] a thing that does work

platform [PLAT-form] a floor

pirates [PIE-ruts] people who steal from ships at sea

treasure [TREH-zhur] anything that is worth a lot of money

tunnel [TUN-ul] a long hole through which people or things can pass

The Money Pit on Oak Island off Nova Scotia has been there at least since 1795. There may be treasure that could be worth millions. But no one has been able to get at it.

In the summer of 1795, three teen-aged lumberjacks took a boat to Oak Island. They walked through the woods to a clearing. The tree in the clearing had odd marks on its trunk. Some of its branches had been cut off short. It looked as though a rope or chain had been thrown over one of the branches. A hollow in the ground under the tree seemed to be about 12 feet across. The lumberjacks thought what you might think. They thought that treasure had been buried there. Since they had nothing to dig with, they went home.

The next morning they came back. With them they had picks and shovels. They started digging in the hollow. Ten feet down, they hit wood. It turned out to be a thick log platform. Under it was dirt. So they kept digging. At 20 feet down, they found another platform. And they found another at 30 feet. That was as deep as they could dig. They were afraid the sides of the hole would fall in on them.

By the time eight years went by, many more people were looking for the treasure. The hole had come to be called the Money Pit. At every ten feet, down to 90 feet, diggers found another oak platform. They also found one piece of very old wire and a couple of ship's whistles. There was some matting, too. It was made from stuff that came from the south. At 90 feet, they came upon a flat stone. The stone had strange writing on it. No one ever figured out what the writing said. And later, the stone was lost.

Then the hole filled with water. No one knew why. So another hole was dug near the first. At 100 feet down, a tunnel was dug from it to the Money Pit. The second hole filled with water.

In 1849, men drilled into the Money Pit to about 100 feet down. The drill went through some layers of interesting stuff: 5 inches of wood, next 12 inches of wood, then 12 inches of nothing, then 4 inches of wood, 22 inches of metal pieces, 8 inches of wood, 22 more inches of metal pieces, and last 10 inches of wood. During the drilling, the men kept bringing up the drill. They wanted to see if anything was sticking to it. Once, something was. Three tiny gold links from a chain were caught in the drill bit. The diggers thought what you would think. There must be a lot more gold down there. They dug deeper.

By now, the diggers knew the water in the Money Pit was salty. It rose and fell with the tide. So they knew that it had to come from the ocean. The people who had buried the treasure had figured out a way that no one but they could get it. They had run a tunnel from the pit to the ocean. But there was probably some kind of gate to keep the water out of the hold. Only the men who buried the treasure knew how to dig it up without letting water in. Others didn't. Others built a dam to keep the ocean out. But the dam fell in. They tried pumps with no luck.

In 1839, drilling went down 154 feet. Down that far was a huge

treasure room, they thought. The drill bit came up with a piece of paper-like stuff. On it were two letters. The letters might have been a *w* and an *i.*

Soon there were pits everywhere on Oak Island. People were digging with a 12-ton machine. They sent down deep-sea divers. They sent down a TV camera. In 1969, a group of people got together to try and get the treasure. So far, they have spent more than $500,000. But they have not found it.

Why hasn't the treasure been dug up? Some people say there is a Pirate's Curse on it. Others say that "Big Dog," the devil's demon, guards it. More think that the people who buried it were just too smart, even for today's machines.

READING QUESTIONS

Choose the best answer. Write in your notebook the number of each question and the letter—a, b, c, or d—that shows the best answer.

1. What is this story mostly about?
    (a) Pirates who buried their treasure
    (b) People who have found buried treasure
    (c) Places buried treasure might be found
    (d) A buried treasure that is difficult to get at

2. When was the Oak Island Money Pit first found?
    (a) 1650
    (b) 1795
    (c) 1900
    (d) 1893

3. What made three lumberjacks think treasure might have been buried on Oak Island?
    (a) A sign that pirates had left
    (b) Three pieces of gold chain
    (c) A story told by an old man
    (d) Marks on a tree and a pit under it

4. What did the lumberjacks find ten feet down?
   (a) A box of gold pieces
   (b) A wooden platform
   (c) A whistle
   (d) A dead man

5. What eventually happened to stop people from going down into the hole?
   (a) The island sank in the ocean.
   (b) The sides of the hole fell in.
   (c) Two men died.
   (d) The hole filled with water.

6. What proof of treasure was found?
   (a) Three gold links
   (b) A piece of gold money
   (c) Letters on paper-like stuff
   (d) Water coming into the pit

7. How did the people who buried the treasure plan to keep others out?
   (a) They made the sides slippery.
   (b) They built a fence.
   (c) They put sharp sticks in the way.
   (d) They ran a tunnel to the ocean.

8. What was on the paper the drill brought up from the Money Pit?
   (a) A list of what was in the pit
   (b) Two letters that looked liked a w and an i
   (c) A note written in strange writing
   (d) The name of one of the people who had buried the treasure

WORDS TO KNOW

Choose the word that best fits the blank in each sentence. Write it in your notebook beside the number of sentence.

**tunnel   machine   pirates   platform   lumberjacks
treasure   camera**

1. People who cut down trees for a living are called _____.

2. The _____ might be gold.

3. The _____ was made of oak.

4. They ran a _____ from the pit to the ocean.

5. A 12-ton _____ wasn't able to get at the treasure.

6. People who steal from ships are called _____.

7. Sending down a TV _____ didn't help.

READING NUMBERS

In this list, some numbers from the story are written in words. Write them on a piece of paper. Then next to each one, write the same number in numerals.

      Example: Fifty-two   52

1. Ninety

2. Ten

3. Seventeen hundred, ninety-five

4. Twenty

5. Thirty

6. One hundred

7. Twenty-two

8. Eighteen hundred, ninety-three

9. One hundred, fifty-four

10. Five hundred thousand

SPEAKING AND LISTENING

Discuss the following questions with your classmates.

1. What made the lumberjacks think treasure was on Oak Island?

2. What did the three gold links promise about what might be in the Money Pit?

3. How did drillers know the water in the pit came from the ocean?

4. Why couldn't drillers get to the treasure?

5. What did the drillers probably think when the drill bit came up with bits of wood in it?

6. What do you think the treasure is? Why?

7. Who buried the treasure? Why?

8. Why might pirates not have the time to dig so deep?

FINDING IT

On a map or globe, find Nova Scotia. How far is it from where you live?

TIME LINE

1795	1803	1849	1893	1969

Copy this time line on a piece of paper. Then write the following items on the time line, according to when they happened at Oak Island.

Drilling went down to 154 feet.
A group of people spent $500,000 trying to get the treasure.
The treasure site was first found.
Drilling went down to 100 feet.
Lumberjacks had been joined by others.

MAKING A DIAGRAM

Copy the diagram on the following page on a piece of paper. Fill in the missing information.

The Money Pit

10 ft. Found: a log platform

20 ft. Found: _____

30 ft. Found: _____

40 ft. Found: _____

50 ft. Found: _____

60 ft. Found: _____

60 ft. Found: _____

70 ft. Found: _____

80 ft. Found: _____

90 ft. Found: _____

100 ft. Found: _____

_____

_____

_____

_____

154 ft. Found: _____

WHAT CAN BE PROVEN?

Copy this outline on a separate piece of paper. Then fill in the blanks, using facts from the story.

A. Things that are true

   1. The lumberjacks found a tree with marks on it.

   2. _____.

   3. _____.

B. Things that we don't know yet but that can be proven if the treasure is reached

   1. Part of the treasure is a box of gold chain.

   2. _____.

   3. _____.

C. Things that probably are not true

   1. There is a Pirate's Curse on the treasure.

   2. _____.

17

CINQUE

WORDS

captured [KAP-churd] taken and kept from escaping

case [KAYS] a matter decided by law

coast [KOHST] the land on the edge of the sea

court [KORT] a place where cases are decided by law

crew [KROO] people who work on a ship

slaves [SLAYVZ] people who are owned by other people

Think of what it would be like to be Cinque. You are a person from Africa, son of a chief. One day, you are captured. You are put in chains. A man whips you on board a ship. You do not know what is happening. Only the other captured people speak your language. For three months, you are at sea. You do not know where you are going. Sometimes you are so sad, you don't want to eat. Besides, the food is very bad. But food is forced down your throat. At last the ship comes to a piece of land.

This piece of land was Cuba. Cuba is an island off the coast of North America. The year was 1839. Cinque and 49 other people from Africa were taken from one ship and put on another. The new ship would take them to another part of Cuba. There they would work as slaves. But none of the Africans knew that.

On the fourth day at sea, Cinque decided he had to know what would happen to him and his friends. For a little while each day, they were let out of their chains. At one of those times, Cinque went to see the ship's cook. In sign language he asked what would happen to them.

The cook knew what Cinque was asking. He was a mean man. He pointed to a pot. The pot was boiling. Cinque knew what the cook meant. The cook was saying that Cinque and his friends would be boiled alive. Of course, this wasn't true. But the cook had to have his joke. It cost him his life.

That night Cinque thought about what to do. A nail in a board gave him an idea. Though he was chained, he was able to work the nail loose. With it he picked the lock on the chains of the man next to him. That man was free. So he could set Cinque free. Soon all the Africans were out of their chains.

At three in the morning, most of the ship's crew were asleep. Only the man who steered the ship was awake. The Africans quietly crawled up the ladder to the deck. With them they carried big knives they had found. With his knife, Cinque killed the captain and the cook. The two slave owners begged for their lives in sign language. Cinque knew he needed them. He and the other Africans did not know how to sail a ship. So he let the two men live. He had no choice. It was the only way they could get back to Africa.

Cinque knew the way they were going by the sun. The slave owners could tell that. So by day, they had the crew sail east, toward Africa. But at night, they turned the ship. They added more sails so they could go faster. And at night they sailed North.

RAFFLE

Mr. Joseph Jennings respectfully informs his friends and the public that, at the request of many acquaintances, he has been induced to purchase from Mr. Osborne, of Missouri, the celebrated

DARK BAY HORSE, "STAR,"

Aged five years, square trotter and warranted sound; with a new light Trotting Buggy and Harness; also, the dark, stout

MULATTO GIRL, "SARAH,"

Aged about twenty years, general house servant, valued at *nine hundred dollars*, and guaranteed, and

Will be Raffled for

At 4 o'clock P. M., February first, at the selection hotel of the subscribers. The above is as represented, and those persons who may wish to engage in the usual practice of raffling, will, I assure them, be perfectly satisfied with their destiny in this affair.

The whole is valued at its just worth, fifteen hundred dollars; fifteen hundred

CHANCES AT ONE DOLLAR EACH.

The Raffle will be conducted by gentlemen selected by the interested subscribers present. Five nights will be allowed to complete the Raffle. BOTH OF THE ABOVE DESCRIBED CAN BE SEEN AT MY STORE, No. 78 Common St., second door from Camp, at from 9 o'clock A. M. to 2 P. M.

Highest throw to take the first choice; the lowest throw the remaining prize, and the fortunate winners will pay twenty dollars each for the refreshments furnished on the occasion.

N. B. No chances recognized unless paid for previous to the commencement.

JOSEPH JENNINGS.

Weeks went by. Food and water were starting to run out. Seven of the Africans had died. Then, 50 days after they left Cuba, the saw land again. It was not Africa. The hearts of the Africans sank. They had been tricked. But they could do nothing. Though they didn't know it, they were off the coast of New York. An American ship captured their ship. Cinque wanted to be free. He dove overboard to get away. It took the Americans an hour to capture him. He and the others were put in jail at first.

Cuba was then owned by Spain. Spain did not allow slave trade. Yet slave trade went on anyway. Spain told the United States it wanted the Africans back. Many Americans did not want to give the Africans to Spain. The case was tried in court. Cinque became famous. His picture was sold in the streets. People came for miles to see him and his friends. The Africans were let out of jail. But they had to wait for the court to finish with the case. While they did, they lived in a small town. In some rooms over a store, they went to school. They learned English. After two years, the Africans won their case. They were free to do what they wanted to do. Of course, they wanted to go back to Africa. By putting on a show, they got enough money to rent a ship. They sailed this ship back home. And they all thanked Cinque, who was brave and smart.

READING QUESTIONS

Choose the best answer. Write in your notebook the number of each question and the letter—a, b, c, or d—that shows the best answer.

1. What is this story mostly about?
    (a) A person who refused to be a slave
    (b) A ship's cook who made a mistake

    (c) A captain who sold slaves for money

    (d) A person who learned to sail a ship

2. Who was Cinque?

    (a) A ship's captain

    (b) A son of an African chief

    (c) A person from Spain

    (d) A person from Cuba

3. What did the cook tell Cinque in sign language?

    (a) That he was a slave

    (b) That he would be boiled

    (c) That he would be taken back to Africa

    (d) That he should kill the captain

4. How did Cinque get out of his chains?

    (a) By picking a chain with a nail

    (b) By bursting them

    (c) By paying the cook

    (d) By jumping overboard

5. Why did Cinque let the two slave owners live?

    (a) He was kind.

    (b) He need them to sail the ship.

    (c) He was a friend of theirs.

    (d) They had knives.

6. How did Cinque know the way they were going?

    (a) By the sun

    (b) By the stars

    (c) By what the cook told him

    (d) By using a compass

7. Why did Cinque sail to the coast of New York?

    (a) The slave owners tricked Cinque.

    (b) Cinque wanted to go there to get water.

(c) Cinque told the crew the wrong directions.

(d) It was Cinque's home.

8. What did Cinque do when the American ship took the ship he was on?

(a) He fought with his knife.

(b) He let it happen.

(c) He jumped overboard to get away.

(d) He called the crew.

WORDS TO KNOW

Choose the word that best fits the blank in each sentence. Write it in your notebook besides the number of the sentence.

case   court   crew   captured   coast   slaves

1. The Africans' _____ was tried in court.

2. The ship landed on the _____ of Africa.

3. Cinque was _____ by the crew.

4. Cinque and his friends were sold as _____.

5. To decide the matter, they took it to _____.

6. The _____ put up the sails.

SPEAKING AND LISTENING

Discuss these questions with your classmates.

1. Cinque was a leader. What might have made him that way? What is the difference between a leader and a follower? Think of a leader you know. What makes that person a leader?

2. Why was Cinque brave? Would he have been as brave if he had not thought he was going to be boiled? What makes you say so?

3. Why did the cook make such a foolish joke?

4. What if you were a lawyer backing Cinque and his friends? What reasons would you give for them to be freed?

5. How long did the slave owners trick Cinque? Why did it take so long to get from Cuba to New York?

SIGN LANGUAGE

Deaf people have a special sign language all their own. Native Americans used sign language to talk to each other. You can try out sign language, too. In a group, have each person write one sentence giving an order. Example: *Go to the door.* Fold the papers and put them in a pile. In turn, have each person in the group pick a paper. Then have that person make up signs and use the signs to give the order to another person. What signs seem to be used over and over? Why?

WRITING OR TELLING A STORY

Write or tell a story about the thoughts of Cinque during one of these times. The story need not be very long. If you write, do it on a separate piece of paper.

1. When he saw the cook point to the pot

2. When he jumped overboard

3. When he found out he was free to go back to Africa

FINDING OUT

1. Find the following places on a map or globe: Africa, Cuba, New York, Spain. How far is it from Africa to Cuba? How far is it from Cuba to New York?

2. Look in an almanac or encyclopedia to find how Spain came to own Cuba.

18

MARY KINGSLEY

PEOPLE

Fans [FANZ] a tribe in Africa
Kiva [KEE-vuh] a Fan leader
Mary Kingsley [MAR-ee KINGZ-lee] a woman from England
Wiki [WEE-kee] a Fan

WORDS

leeches [LEE-chuz] worms that suck blood
rubber [RUB-er] material made from sticky juice of a plant

trader [TRAY-der] a person who makes a living by giving one thing in return for another

umbrella [um-BREL-uh] a thing for keeping the rain off

Mary Kingsley's dream was to travel in wild places. Her dream came true. She learned science. Because of that, she got a chance to go from England, where she lived, to Africa. Mary's job was to collect strange fish. She also was a trader. She traded things like cloth and fish hooks for rubber and elephant teeth.

161

PART I

The place where Mary was in Africa was quiet. Mary wanted to take a trip. She wanted to go up the river. There lived the Fans, her favorite tribe of people. She liked the Fans because they were lively and friendly. People told her not to go up the river. The trip would be full of danger, they said. The tribes were about to go to war. Mary didn't care. She decided to go anyhow.

First she learned to paddle a canoe well. Then she hired some African helpers. All had guns. They took off in a canoe. At first the ride was easy and beautiful. Around them, other Africans paddled canoes full of fruit. Birds sang.

Then the land changed. Something about it was scary. All was quiet. Silver bubbles rose in the water as the canoe paddles struck it. At last they came to a large island. Fans lived there. The

Fans came pouring down a hill on the island. They were carrying guns and knives. They did not look friendly.

Mary went on shore. The faces around her looked angry. She greeted the Fans in their language. They did not answer her. Soon a man came down through the crowd. Mary could tell he was a leader. From his shoulder hung wildcat tails. His name, she found out later, was Kiva.

One of the men with Mary rushed up to Kiva. He stopped just short of Kiva and held his hand a little away from him. This was a Fan salute. "Don't you know me, my friend? he asked.

Kiva raised his hands to show he did know the man. Then another of Mary's group saw a friend, and another. Mary looked around for someone she knew. All were strangers. "It was touch-and-go for twenty of the longest minutes I had ever lived," she said later.

The Fans had never seen anything like Mary. She wore a

long dress. With her she carried an umbrella, even when it wasn't raining. No one dressed like that in Fan country. But the Fans decided she was all right. They gave her a hut to sleep in for the night. The next day she hired four Fans to go up the river with her. One was Kiva. Another man was called Wiki.

Through a forest thick with vines, they walked up along the river. The first day they went 25 miles. Every two hours the Fans stopped to eat. The other dropped behind. Mary walked between the Fans and the others. Once she saw five elephants taking a bath in the mud. She ran to Kiva and said she thought an elephant hunt might be fun. He said no. There were not enough people in the group to hunt elephants.

Then they started uphill. In some places, old trees had fallen. While walking over the trees, which lay on their sides, Mary and the others would sometimes slip and fall. They would fall down between the branches. Snakes lived down there. Then others would pull them up with vine ropes. It was dark before they got even near the village they were trying to reach.

READING QUESTIONS

Choose the best answer. Write in your notebook the number of each question and the letter—a, b, c, or d—that shows the best answer.

1. How can Mary Kingsley best be described?
   (a) As quiet
   (b) As funny
   (c) As brave
   (d) As slow

2. What had Mary Kingsley studied, mainly?
   (a) Language
   (b) History
   (c) Science
   (d) Music

3. What did Mary Kingsley want to hunt?
   (a) Elephants
   (b) Monkeys
   (c) Tigers
   (d) Antelope

4. What did Mary Kingsley usually carry?
   (a) A stick
   (b) A gun
   (c) An axe
   (d) An umbrella

5. Where does the story say that snakes lived?
   (a) Under fallen trees
   (b) In dark caves
   (c) Beside the swamp
   (d) On the mountain

6. Why was Mary Kingsley's trip dangerous?
   (a) Disease had struck the area.
   (b) War was about to begin.
   (c) Storms were sweeping the jungle.
   (d) There was a plague of rats.

7. What was one of the things Mary Kingsley brought to Africa to trade?
   (a) Guns
   (b) Belts
   (c) Jewelry
   (d) Fish hooks

8. On the water, how did Mary Kingsley travel?
   (a) On a raft
   (b) In a canoe
   (c) In a rowboat
   (d) On a sailboat

PART II

It was so dark that the path was not clear. It seemed to stop at one place. Then it started in again on the other side of some brush. It would have been wise to go around the brush. But Mary was tired. She walked straight ahead. It was a mistake. Suddenly she fell into a deep hole. The hole was a trap the Fans had dug to catch big animals. At the bottom were wooden sticks sticking up. But Mary was lucky. She had a good thick skirt on. She was not hurt.

"Get a rope. Get me out!" she called.

One of the men asked, "You killed?"

"Not much," Mary answered. "Get a rope and pull me out."

Nothing happened for a long time. She could hear the men talking. Then Wiki went to get a vine for a rope. Down in the hole, Mary felt far from England. It was dark. She thought that maybe they would leave her there. Maybe they didn't like her, after all. More time went by. She looked at the smooth yellow walls of the hole. The walls slanted in toward the top. She tried to think of a way to climb out.

When she was about to give up on the men, they came to pull her out. The group went on to the village. The people there were not very friendly. So after a night's rest, Mary's group went on. In the next village, the people tied Kiva up. He owed something to one of the people. A group of village people got together in a group to decide what to do. Mary sat in on it. She learned to say, "Azuna!" That means, "Silence! I am talking!" In the end, she paid what Kiva owed. The people let him go.

The next day she saw five gorillas eating leaves. She was with Wiki. To keep Wiki from shooting the gorillas, she put her hand on his shoulder. He didn't know what she meant. He thought she wanted him to shoot them. So he grabbed Mary's wrist. He did that to show her he didn't want to kill the gorillas. Then Wiki made an odd sound. He grabbed his throat. His head rolled. Mary didn't know what was wrong with him. Then he put his face in some dried leaves. And he sneezed! The sound scared the gorillas. They made a noise something between a bark and a howl. And off they went.

Trading at each village, the group went on. They heard that one village had made a rule to shoot strangers on sight. So they went around that village. That way led them into a wet place. Twice they were in water over their heads. Leeches stuck to their necks. The leeches sucked their blood. Later, on dry land, they had to pull the leeches off.

After Mary had found enough fishes and traded enough goods, she decided to go back down the river. The trip back was easy. She floated down the river in a canoe.

Home in England, Mary fought for African rights. Parts of Africa had been taken by England. English rulers in Africa made Africans follow English law. Mary tried to tell the English that African law was just as good. She wrote books about Africa. Some people listened to her. They could tell she was right. Others thought she was strange. But she went her own way.

READING QUESTIONS

Choose the best answer. Write in your notebook the number of each question and the letter—a, b, c, or d—that shows the best answer.

1. What is this story mostly about?
   (a) The adventures of a person who explored Africa
   (b) The way some people in Africa make a living
   (c) The way wars are fought by people in Africa
   (d) The different kinds of animals that are found in Africa

2. How did Mary get to go to Africa?
   (a) She got a job using her ability to speak Fan.
   (b) She got a job using her knowledge of science.
   (c) She got a job as servant to some rich people.
   (d) She got a job as tour guide with a company.

3. Why did some people think Mary would be in danger if she went up the river?
   (a) The country was wild.
   (b) There were fallen trees.
   (c) No one had been there.
   (d) There might be wars.

4. How did Mary's men greet the Fans?
   (a) With a Fan salute
   (b) By saying "Azuna!"
   (c) By shaking hands
   (d) By saying hello

5. What happened to Kiva at one of the Fan villages?
   (a) He was beaten up.
   (b) He was tied up.
   (c) He was killed.
   (d) He was given strange fish.

6. How did the matter of what Kiva owed get settled?
   (a) Mary paid it.
   (b) They fought it out.
   (c) It was taken to the English courts.
   (d) Kiva was killed.

7. What did Mary do when she got back to England?
   (a) She took it easy.
   (b) She wrote books about her trip.
   (c) She opened a store.
   (d) She traded with the English.

8. What did she tell the English about the Africans?
   (a) That the Africans were wild
   (b) That the Africans were always making war
   (c) That the Africans liked her
   (d) That the Africans had good laws

WORDS TO KNOW

Choose the word that best fits the blank in each sentence. Write it in your notebook beside the number of the sentence.

umbrella   rubber   leeches   trader

1. Mary always carried an _____, even when it wasn't raining.

2. She traded fish hooks and cloth for _____ and elephant teeth.

3. When Mary's group went in the water, _____ sucked their blood.

4. One of Mary's jobs was to be a _____.

SPEAKING AND LISTENING

Discuss these questions with your classmates.

1. How were Mary and Cinque alike? How were they different?

2. What made Mary want to go to wild paces? Would she have gotten to Africa if she hadn't done things to make it happen? What did she do to make it happen?

3. What kind of people were the Fans? How do you know?

4. What is one way the Fans got their food? What might they do if a leopard fell in the trap?

5. What tells you Mary was a brave woman?

6. How did she help the Africans when she got back to England?

7. What do you dream of doing? How could you make it happen?

MAKING A MAP

On a separate piece of paper, make up a map showing where Mary went in Africa. Be sure to put in the river and the villages.

FINDING IT

On a map or globe, find Africa and England.How far is it from England to Africa? Mary went to Africa about 100 years ago. How might she have gotten there?

CLASSIFYING

Leopards and elephants belong to the class *animals*. Often the writer of a book will give you clues about the meaning of a word by telling you its class. For example:

1. A leopard is an animal with spots.

2. An elephant is an animal that is very large and has a trunk.

In each case, the writer has told you that she or he is talking about something that belongs to the class *animals*. The sentences also give details about the animals. One tells you that the leopard is an animal *with spots*, for example. When you read such sentences, you can learn the meaning of new words.

Write these sentences on a separate piece of paper. Then fill in the blanks with one of the following words that tell the class.

place   animal   tool

1. An apartment is a _____ where people live.

2. A fish is an _____ that lives in water.

3. A pen is a _____ that is used for writing.

4. Skateboarding is a _____ using a wheeled board.

5. A nest is a _____ where a bird lays eggs.

6. A hammer is a _____ used to drive nails.

7. A water ouzel is an _____ that flies under water.

8. A knife is a _____ used to cut things up.

DRAWING A CARTOON STRIP

On a piece of paper, draw a comic strip showing one of these things:

1. Mary telling the leopard to go home

2. Mary trying to get out of the trap

MAKING UP A LIST

Write a list of things you could do to make a dream of yours come true.

19

MUMMIES

PERSON

Thomas Pettigrew [TAHM-us PET-uh-groo] a doctor who lived in the 1800s

WORDS

mummy [MUM-ee] a dried body of a dead person
onion [UN-yun] a kind of vegetable
robbers [ROB-erz] people who steal
tomb [TOOM] a room where a dead person is put

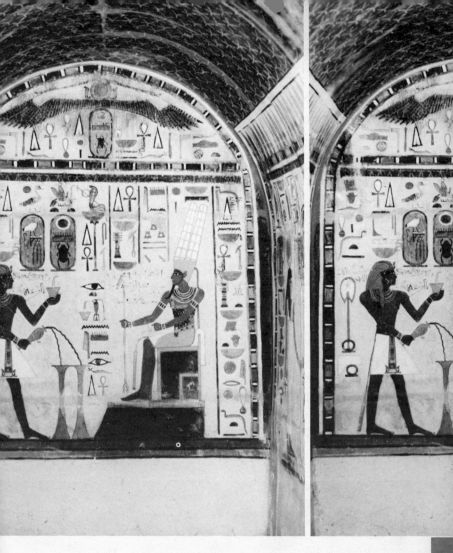

Egypt is a country in Africa. Thousands of years ago, life there was very good for rich people. Kings were called gods. They lived in great houses. Slaves fanned them in the heat. Their food was tasty. Good times were many. In fact, life was so good that the Egyptians planned to live forever. That's why they made mummies of the dead.

Egyptians thought that each person had a spirit called Ba. After a person died, Ba left the body. At night it went to another world. In the day it came back to the tomb. There it would rest and eat. Sometimes the spirit went back inside the body. If it couldn't do that, it might go into an animal's body and drive it crazy.

It was important that the spirit have a body to go to. And it was also important that the name of the body be known. If not, the spirit might not be able to find the right body. So first the body had to be kept in good shape. The hot, dry weather in Egypt was a help. Because of it, things didn't rot so fast there. But Egyptians had ways of keeping bodies even longer. They took out the body's insides and put them in jars. Then they covered the body with natron (NAY-trahn), a mineral powder. The body was stuffed with various things: sawdust, onions, cloth. It was rubbed with oil. Then it was wrapped in hundreds of yards of cloth.

The body, now a mummy, was dried. Holy words were said over it. Then it was put in a tomb. The name of the per-

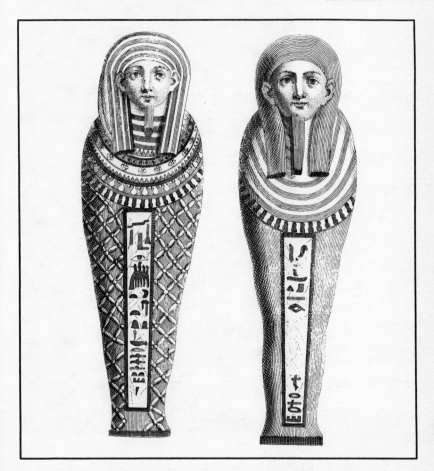

son was written everywhere so the spirit could find it. Everything the person might need in another life was put in the tomb: food, money, jewels, gold. Games were put in the tomb for the spirit to play with when things got dull. One king even had a big boat in his tomb.

Egyptian tombs were setups for grave robbers. To keep robbers out, some kings blocked their tombs with rocks. Some of those rocks weighed as much as 45 tons. The robbers got in anyhow.

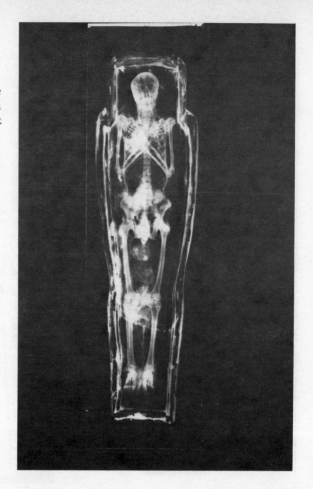

Today mummies are X-rayed so they can be studied without damaging them.

People robbed the tombs for more than riches. Doctors in early days gave ground-up mummy to people who were sick. This often made them sicker. You can see why. Other people made paper from mummy cloth.

In the 1800s, mummies were a fad. Dr. Thomas Pettigrew made a good thing out of this fad. His nickname was Mummy. He bought mummies from Egypt. Then he sold tickets to a mummy unwrapping in a big hall. Hundreds would come to watch him unwrap the mummy from its cloth. When he did this, Pettigrew didn't know what he would find. Once, he unwrapped a mummy covered with gold. Another of his mummies had an onion in its hand. And once, he unwrapped a mummy only to find a trick had been played on him. Inside those yards of cloth were sawdust, a stick, and part of a cat's backbone.

Today we treat mummies better. Experts x-ray mummies to see what's under the cloth. They have found some interesting things:

1. One wore a wig to cover a bald spot.
2. A whole family of mummies had buck teeth.
3. A king had a bad case of blackheads.
4. Another king was hit over the head and died from it.
5. One queen had an ape buried with her. Some think she died having a baby, but the baby lived. So they buried the ape with her in place of the baby.

READING QUESTIONS

Choose the best answer. Write in your notebook the number of each question and the letter—a, b, c, or d—that shows the best answer.

1. What is the story mostly about?
   (a) The weather in Egypt
   (b) The history of Egypt
   (c) The mummies of Egypt
   (d) The ruins in Egypt
2. What is a mummy?
   (a) An old man
   (b) A spirit
   (c) A dried body
   (d) A doctor

3. Why was the name of the mummy written in so many places?
   (a) So the people would know who it was
   (b) Because the Egyptians thought a lot of themselves
   (c) Because the kings said to do it
   (d) So the spirit could find the body

4. How were mummies used in the early days by doctors?
   (a) They were used to show others how to dry bodies.
   (b) They were opened up.
   (c) They were brought back to life.
   (d) They were ground up and given to sick people.

5. Where did Pettigrew get his mummies?
   (a) From Canada
   (b) From Egypt
   (c) From Iran
   (d) From England

6. What trick was played on Pettigrew?
   (a) Other things were put in the wrappings of one mummy.
   (b) A cat jumped out of the mummy wrappings.
   (c) One of the mummies had an onion in its hand.
   (d) Ground-up mummy was put in his tea.

7. How do experts find out about mummies today?
   (a) They unwrap them.
   (b) They x-ray them.
   (c) They cut them up.
   (d) They dye them with colors.

8. What did the experts find out about a whole family of mummies?
   (a) They all had buck teeth.
   (b) They all had blackheads.
   (c) They all wore wigs.
   (d) They all ate onions.

WORDS TO KNOW

Choose the word that best fits the blank in each sentence. Write it in your notebook beside the number of the sentence.

mummy   onion   robbers   tomb

1. The mummy had an _____ in its hand.
2. The Egyptians put the mummy in its _____ after the holy words were said.
3. A _____ is a dried body.
4. The _____ stole the gold and jewels.

SPEAKING AND LISTENING

Discuss these questions with your classmates.

1. What did the Egyptians believe about life after death? How might we know this? How is it like what you believe? How is it different?
2. What do we do with dead bodies? Why?
3. Why is it important to find out about mummies? What else might we find out from x-raying them?
4. Why do you think the ape was buried with the queen? Does anyone know the reason for sure? Why?

CHANGING _Y_ TO _I_ AND ADDING _ES_

The word meaning "more than one mummy" is *mummies*. To make the word *mummies*, the *y* on *mummy* was changed to *i*, and then *es* was added. Many words ending in *y* are changed to words that mean more than one in this way.

On a separate piece of paper, write the following words, changing them to mean more than one. (Not all will have the *i* changed to *y* and *es* added.) Then use each word in a sentence.

robber   country   spirit

body   word

IN WHAT ORDER?

The following is a list of what the Egyptians did to make a mummy. The steps are *not* in the order in which they were done. On a piece of paper, write the list so that the steps are in the right order.

The body was stuffed.

Natron was put on the body.

The body was put in a tomb.

Holy words were said over the body.

The body's insides were taken out.

The body was wrapped with cloth.

The body's insides were put in jars.

Food for another life was put in the tomb.

The name of the person was written everywhere.

The body was dried.

HOW IS IT DONE?

The story tells how a mummy was made. In order to do it, certain things were done in a certain order. Out loud or in writing, tell how to do something. For example, you might tell how to do one of the following things. If you write the steps, do it on a separate piece of paper.

1. Tie a shoelace
2. Wrap a present
3. Start a car
4. Put a car in gear
5. Make a dress
6. Sew on a button

LOOKING IT UP

Look up one of the following subjects. On a piece of paper, write a paragraph telling about it.

1. King Tut
2. Egypt
3. The pyramids

THINKING ABOUT SCIENCE

In what ways are things preserved and kept from going bad? Think about food. Tell how one of these ways works to preserve food.

FINDING IT

Find Egypt on a map or globe. What other countries is it near?

unit
4

THE POWERS
of MIND,
MEDICINE,
and MAGIC

20

FIRE WALKERS

PLACES

India [IN-dee-uh] a large country in Asia

Fiji Islands [FEE-jee EYE-lundz] islands in the Pacific Ocean

WORDS

crime [KRIME] an act that is against the law

crops [KROPS] things farmers grow

fire walkers [FIUR WAW-kerz] people who can walk on hot coals or
stones

guilty [GIL-tee] having done something wrong

In India and the Fiji Islands, some people know how to walk on red-hot stones. They do not get hurt. Their feet don't burn. This story tells about one time when people walked on red-hot stones.

It is not time for the fire walkers to start yet. But people are already coming to watch. They sit on a hill. Down below the hill is a pit. The pit is very large. In it are stones covered with burning logs. The logs have been heating up the stones since morning.

185

The chief gives a sign. When he does, 12 men go to
the pit. They are in pairs. Each pair holds a long vine rope
across the pit. One of the pair is on one side. The other of
the pair is on the other side. They walk across the pit,
holding the vine over it. Then the vine catches one of the
logs. They drag the log out, using the vine. Soon all the
logs are gone from the pit. Only the hot stones are left.
The 12 men poke the stones with a stick. They make sure
that all the stones are flat. If points were sticking up, a fire
walker could trip and fall. One of the sticks the men are

poking with breaks. It falls into the pit on the red-hot stones. In 30 seconds it is on fire. What would it be like for a person to fall on the stones?

Then it is time for the fire walkers. From a hut come eight men. They have eaten nothing for 24 hours. They feel that will make them strong in spirit. Their legs and feet are bare. Slowly and very straightly, they walk to the pit. Then they step down on the red-hot stones. Step by step, still moving slowly, they walk around the pit. Not one of them stops. Not one makes a noise. Not one shows pain. When they come out, their feet are not burned at all.

Not all fire walkers get off so easily. Sometimes the magic—whatever it is—does not work. Their feet do get burned. But not as often as you might think.

No one knows why fire walkers don't get burned. Perhaps they know of something to put on their skin. Perhaps they eat or drink something that does the trick.

Probably their feet sweat. The sweat puts a layer of moisture between the stones and their feet. Each time they lift their feet more sweat forms. The sweat protects their feet. But they better not stand too long in one spot.

Why do fire walkers walk on the hot stones? Some do it because they believe it will make for better crops. Others just do it because they have said they will. Still others walk on the stones to show they are not guilty of some crime. The people in their group believe that only the guilty will burn. The not guilty will go unhurt.

READING QUESTIONS

Choose the best answer. Write in your notebook the number of each question and the letter—a, b, c, or d—that shows the best answer.

1. What is this story mostly about?
    (a) How people who live in India and the Fiji Islands earn money
    (b) A strange custom of some people in India and the Fiji Islands
    (c) Beliefs people in India and the Fiji Islands have about religion
    (d) How people in India and the Fiji Islands celebrate a holiday

2. What do the people use to heat the red-hot stones?
    (a) Logs
    (b) Coal
    (c) Gas
    (d) Paper

3. Where are the red-hot stones that some people walk on?
    (a) Up on a hill
    (b) Down in a pit
    (c) In the woods
    (d) In a house

4. What event in the story shows that the stones are hot?
   (a) A bird was roasted.
   (b) A stick burst into flames.
   (c) A man fell and died.
   (d) A person got burned.

5. What do the fire walkers do before walking on the hot stones?
   (a) Exercise
   (b) Fight
   (c) Eat meat
   (d) Eat nothing

6. How do the fire walkers walk in the pit?
   (a) Slowly
   (b) With a dance step
   (c) With a yell
   (d) Very fast

7. What is one reason mentioned as to why fire walkers don't get burned?
   (a) Their feet sweat.
   (b) They drink a magic potion.
   (c) They put water on the stones.
   (d) They are doctors.

8. What is one reason the fire walkers agree to walk on hot coals?
   (a) To make people obey them
   (b) To become king
   (c) To show they are not guilty of something
   (d) To gain the ability to fly

WORDS TO KNOW

Choose the word that best fits the blank in each sentence. Write it in your notebook beside the number of the sentence.

fire walkers   crime   crops   guilty

1. It is a _____ to steal.
2. A robber is _____ of a crime.
3. The _____ walk on red-hot stones.
4. Farmers grow _____.

SPEAKING AND LISTENING

Discuss these questions with your classmates.

1. What do you think keeps the fire walkers from getting burned?

2. Can you think of other things people do that are hard to explain? What are they? Why might people do them? How might they be done?

3. Do you think fire walking can help crops grow? How? Do you think it might show who is guilty of something? How?

4. Have you ever done anything to prove yourself? What was it? Were you able to go through with it? Was it worth it?

5. Can you believe everything you see? Why or why not?

WRITING ABOUT THOUGHTS AND FEELINGS

Write three sentences on a piece of paper telling about one of these:

1. A fire walker's feelings before walking on the red-hot stones

2. A fire walker's thoughts while walking on the red-hot stones

3. The thoughts of a child watching a parent walking on the stones

21

BURIED ALIVE! –
HARRY HOUDINI

PERSON

Erich Weiss [ER-ik WEIS] the name Houdini was given at birth

WORDS

control [kun-TROHL] have power over

escaped [es-KAYPD] get out of

magician [muh-JISH-un] a person who does magic tricks

rabbi [RAB-ie] a Jewish leader

His name was Erich Weiss. He was the son of a rabbi. At the age of six, he could pick locks. One lock he picked was on the place where his mother kept pies. She put a stop to that. But Erich kept trying to pick locks. He learned other tricks. When he was nine, he did tricks for the circus. After he was grown up, he changed his name to Harry Houdini (hoo-DEE-nee). He became a famous magician. One of the things he did was to be buried alive and live through it!

Harry came near the open hole in the empty lot. The people cheered. Many were afraid to think of what was about to happen. But still they stayed. It was just too good to miss. Harry would be buried alive. He would lie in a box under six feet of ground. He would be there for nearly an hour. When the box was brought back up, would he still be alive?

Could he do it? If anyone could, he could. A short time before he had escaped from jail. Harry was not in jail for doing something wrong. The only time he had ever got caught doing wrong was when he took those pies. It was a lucky thing that he didn't do anything wrong. For there

Houdini does his stunt of escaping from a straight jacket.

wasn't a jail that could hold him. Harry would let people lock him in a jail cell. Then he would pick the lock to get out as a trick. And that wasn't all. Tied with ropes, he had jumped into rivers. Underwater he had gotten out of the ropes. No one knew how he did it.

Now straight as a tree, Harry stood proudly. He had a right to be proud. For he could do things no one else in the world could do.

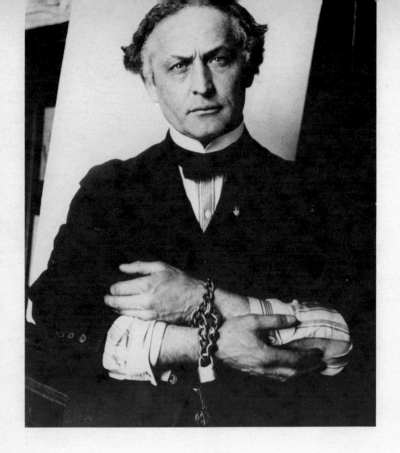

He spoke to the crowd. He told how he would do what he was going to do. The secrets were these: to control his mind so he was not afraid and to take short breaths. He talked about how many hours he had practiced holding his breath.

As he spoke by the dark hole, people thought of what it would be like to be buried alive; to be put in a small place, not able to get out; to lie under six feet of heavy ground; maybe to run out of air and die.

Harry kept talking. Were these words his last?

Then he lay down in the box. Someone closed the lid. Using ropes, men let the box down slowly into the deep hole. They began to shovel the dirt in. Harry could hear the dirt hit the top of the box. He was alone.

The men were to start digging Harry out after 50 minutes. By then he might be running out of air. Time went by slowly. Think of it—50 minutes. That was 3,000 seconds. Every second seemed longer than it should be.

Then at last it was time. The men picked up their shovels and started to dig Harry out. The people moved around and whispered. Could Harry hear the sounds of the shovel? Could he hear nothing at all? Was he dead?

At last the men got to the box. Using ropes they quickly brought it to the top of the hole. Then they set it down on the ground. Someone took the lid off the box. For a minute, nothing happened. Then Harry, looking white, sat up in the box. Slowly he stood. The people broke into a cheer. Harry Houdini had done it again!

READING QUESTIONS

Choose the best answer. Write in your notebook the number of each question and the letter—a, b, c, or d—that shows the best answer.

1. Which of the following titles best fits this story?
    (a) Houdini Escapes from Jail
    (b) Houdini Is Buried Alive
    (c) Houdini Does Tricks for the Circus
    (d) Houdini Opens Any Lock

2. What was Harry's name when he was a boy?
    (a) Harry Houdini
    (b) Harry Weiss
    (c) Erich Weiss
    (d) Erich Houdini

3. How old was Harry when he started doing tricks for the circus?
    (a) Six
    (b) Nine

    (c) Twenty

    (d) Twenty-one

4. How long was the box buried?

    (a) Over an hour

    (b) 50 minutes

    (c) 20 minutes

    (d) 10 minutes

5. Why was Harry put in jail?

    (a) To show a trick

    (b) For stealing pies

    (c) For having jumped in a river

    (d) To be safe from harm

6. What was one of Harry's secrets for being buried alive?

    (a) Breathing control

    (b) An oxygen tank

    (c) An air vent

    (d) A secret tunnel

7. How many feet down was Harry buried?

    (a) Two feet

    (b) Six feet

    (c) Ten feet

    (d) Twelve feet

8. How did the box get buried?

    (a) Harry did it.

    (b) A tractor pushed dirt on it.

    (c) Men shoveled dirt on it.

    (d) A truck dumped dirt on it.

WORDS TO KNOW

Choose the word that best fits the blank in each sentence. Write it in your notebook beside the number of the sentence.

escaped   magician   rabbi   control

1. Harry Houdini knew how to _____ his breathing.

2. He was a famous _____.

3. His father was a _____.

4. Harry Houdini _____ from jail by opening the lock.

SPEAKING AND LISTENING

Discuss these questions with your classmates.

1. Some people thought Harry Houdini knew magic. But all he knew was how to control his mind and how to work fast. Also there were some tricks in what he did. Was the "buried alive" trick magic? Why?

2. What would be the hardest thing to face in being buried alive?

3. What other tricks had Harry done? How might he have done them without magic?

4. Have you seen a magician work? If so, tell about it.

5. Can you do any magic? If so, what trick do you know?

WORDS THAT TELL ABOUT A KIND OF PERSON

What kind of person do you think Harry Houdini was? Think of a word that tells what kind of person he was. You might choose *brave*, or you might choose *smart*. Write your word on a separate piece of paper. Now find three sentences in the story that prove what you said. Write them on the paper, too.

SHOWING A MAGIC TRICK

From a book or a person, learn how to do a magic trick. Then show it to the class or a group. When you are done, tell the secret of the trick.

WRITING STEPS

Write down the steps to a magic trick. Or, write the steps to something else you know how to do. Write the steps in the order in which they should be done.

22

THE MAGIC FORCE: MESMER

PLACE
  Paris [PAR-is] a city in France

PEOPLE
  Friedrich Mesmer [FREED-rich MEZ-mer] a man who lived in the 1700s
  Maria Paradis [muh-REE-uh pah-ruh-DEES] a woman who lived in the 1700s

WORDS
  hypnosis [hyp-NOH-sis] a state like sleep
  magnet [MAG-nut] something able to pull iron and certain other things to itself

magnetism [MAG-nuh-tiz-um] the power in a magnet

suggestion [sug-JEST-chun] something someone suggests or
advises; influence by hypnosis

The man's name was Friedrich Mesmer. He was a doctor who lived in Europe from 1733 to 1815. He thought he had power in his hands and eyes. It was a power he did not claim to understand. He thought it might have come from the stars. Or it might have been some kind of magnetism. Mesmer could make some people well. He did it by using what today is called hypnosis.

Maria Paradis was good at playing music. But, from the time she was a baby, she had been blind. Doctors had tried to cure her. None had been able to. Then along came Mesmer. Mesmer hypnotized Maria and she could see for the first time since she was small. When she was blind, she had forgotten what the world looked like. It was a surprise. She said she liked the way dogs looked. In fact, dogs looked better to her than people did! Maria had been getting money for being blind. Her parents were afraid the money would be cut off now that she could see. So they would not let Mesmer continue seeing her. Without him, Maria went blind again.

For part of his life, Mesmer worked in Paris. He treated people there. Every other day, he treated poor people for free. Some of those who came to him got well.

The place where Mesmer worked was quite a scene. A band played happy music. Mesmer wore long, flowing robes. In his hand, he carried a wand. He kept pointing his wand at the sick people who came to him. Sometimes he stared into their eyes. His eyes pinned them down. They could not look away. They became hypnotized.

In the room where Mesmer worked was a big tub. It was partly filled with water. In the water were tiny pieces of iron and glass. Bottles were in it, too. The small bottles at the edge pointed their necks toward a bigger bottle in the middle. From the tub came cords. At the end of each cord was an iron bar.

Sick people tied the cords around themselves. Sometimes one of Mesmer's helpers held the bars on the places where people were sick. Other times the sick people did it themselves. If a sick person had a headache, the bar was held to the head. If the person's leg hurt, the bar was held to the leg. Mesmer—and everyone else—thought there was a force in the iron bars. The force, they said, was magnetism. The magnetism (they thought) was made in the big tub. Then it went down the cords into the iron bars. When it touched the body, the magnetism supposedly cured whatever was wrong.

There were those who did not like what Mesmer was doing. They thought it was black magic, and they said so. Experts came together. They wanted to see what there was to Mesmer's cures. They decided that the cures were not real because they came from people's minds. Mesmer was kicked out of Paris. The "experts" won.

In those days people did not understand hypnosis. Mesmer, himself, thought the cures came from magnetism. He thought that by doing his "magic" he made the force of magnetism flow. But he was really using hypnosis. He told people they would get well and they *did* get well. The iron bars had nothing to do with it, nor did the big tub, nor the bottles. It was Mesmer's power of suggestion to people that helped them. Since that time, hypnosis has been used by doctors. And we are not sure, even now, how it works.

READING QUESTIONS

Choose the best answer. Write in your notebook the number of each question and the letter—a, b, c, or d—that shows the best answer.

1. What is this story mostly about?
   (a) A doctor who used hypnosis
   (b) A blind person who was made to see
   (c) Different ways hypnosis can be used
   (d) Beliefs people have about hypnosis

2. When did Mesmer live?
   (a) About 1610
   (b) About 1630
   (c) About 1790
   (d) About 1880

3. What did Mesmer think his power was?
   (a) A kind of magnetism
   (b) A kind of light ray
   (c) A kind of radio wave
   (d) A kind of drug

4. What did Mesmer do for Maria Paradis?
   (a) He made her headache go away.
   (b) He made her parents leave her alone.
   (c) He made her see again.
   (d) He made her walk again.

5. What did Mesmer use to treat groups of sick people?
   (a) His robe
   (b) Lotions
   (c) Pills
   (d) A big tub

6. What was in Mesmer's tub?
   (a) Iron, glass, and bottles
   (b) Grass, sticks, and stones

(c) Leaves, mud, and hair
(d) Sugar, lemons, and potatoes

7. What did Mesmer's helpers do for someone with a headache?
   (a) They held a bar to the person's head.
   (b) They gave the person a magnet.
   (c) They said magic words over the person.
   (d) They told the person to forget the headache.

8. How did Mesmer really cure people?
   (a) He used magic on them.
   (b) He used a kind of hypnosis on them.
   (c) He used a magnet on them.
   (d) He used force from the stars on them.

WORDS TO KNOW

Choose the word that best fits the blank in each sentence. Write it in your notebook beside the number of the sentence.

suggestion   magnetism   hypnosis   magnet

1. Mesmer's magic was really the power of _____.
2. Mesmer's power of suggestion was a kind of _____.
3. A _____ pulls iron to it.
4. The power to pull iron is called _____.

SPEAKING AND LISTENING

Discuss these questions with your classmates.

1. Why might Mesmer not have understood what force he was dealing with? Can you think of some forces people don't understand completely yet? What are they?
2. Why does hypnosis work? Have you ever been hypnotized? What was it like?

3.   What is hypnosis used for today?

4.   Why do you think Mesmer put iron in the big tub?

5.   Why was Mesmer right when he said the cures came from nature? Why were the experts right when they said the cures were in people's minds?

6.   What is "suggestion"? Can you think of a time when suggestion was used on you? What was the suggestion? How do people who make up TV ads use suggestion?

7.   What is behind a lot of magic? If people understood everything about magic, would it still be magic?

WORD ENDINGS -IZE AND -ION

The ending -ize makes the word *magnet* into *magnetize*. A magnet is something that pulls iron to it. To magnetize something is to turn it into a magnet. So the ending -ize can mean "turn into" or "cause to become."

The ending -ion makes the word suggest into suggestion. A suggestion is something that someone suggested. It is the result of suggesting. So the ending -ion can mean "result of an act."

Figure out the meaning of the following words. Then write the sentences on a separate piece of paper. Fill in each blank with a word that fits.

realize   construction   magnetize

action   terrorize   suggestion

humanize

1. After thinking about it for a long time, he made a
   _____.

2. The builders are working on some new _____.

3. That gang will _____ the little children.

4. See if you can _____ that piece of iron.

5. It takes a long time to _____ something you only dream of.

6. We've done nothing for too long, so let's have some _____!

7. Is it possible to _____ a wild animal?

SHOWING IT

In two to three minutes, show what magnets can do. Take some time first to read about magnets in a science text. You might want to make a diagram to help you show what magnets can do.

DRAWING A CARTOON STRIP

On a piece of paper, draw a cartoon strip of Mesmer curing people. Put in the tub and the cords. Use balloons to show what people say. Draw four or five cartoon frames.

FINDING IT

Find the city of Paris on a map. Paris is in France. France is in Europe.

WRITING A STORY

Imagine you are Maria Paradis. You are seeing the world for the first time since you were a baby. What does everything look like to you? Write two or three sentences to answer this question.

23

ANNA O.

PLACES

    Austria [AU-stree-uh] a country in central Europe

    Vienna [vee-EN-uh] a city in Austria

PERSON

    Dr. Breuer [Dok-ter BROI-er] a doctor who lived in Vienna; he
    helped discover psychoanalysis

WORDS

    guilt [GILT] a bad feeling with thoughts of having done something
    wrong; or having done something considered wrong

psychoanalysis [sie-koh-uh-NAL-uh-sis] a way of treating sickness of
the mind by having people talk about themselves

patient [PAY-shunt] a person a doctor is treating

undergo [un-der-GOH] pass through; have something done

The year was 1880. The place was Vienna, a city in Austria. A
young woman started to get sick. Her doctor later wrote a
book about her. In it he called her Anna O.

For months, Anna O. had been helping take care of her very sick father. Night after night, she sat by his bedside. One night, she thought he was asleep. She watched him and wondered if he would die. Tears came into her eyes at the awful idea. Suddenly her father spoke. "What time is it?" he asked. Anna tried to blink back the tears. She didn't want her father to see her cry. If he did, he might guess how sick he was. She picked up a watch from the bed table. She couldn't see it clearly. The tears in her eyes made it blur. She brought it closer to her face. It seem huge. The tears made it bigger. She half closed her eyes to see better. It was quarter to twelve.

Another time, she fell asleep in the chair. When she woke, she felt guilty. She was supposed to be awake to keep watch over her father. Then she saw something. She saw a black snake on the wall behind her father's bed. It wasn't really there, but she thought it was. She wanted to stop it from biting her father. She tried to raise her arm. But her arm wouldn't move. It was asleep because it had been across the back of her chair. To her, each finger looked like a little black snake. And each fingernail looked like a death's head. After that, she saw snakes everywhere. Bent sticks looked like snakes to her. So did ropes.

Then Anna O. got sick. She could not move her legs. She could not move her right arm. Her neck would not turn. Her eyes blurred so that she could not read or write. All she would eat was oranges. At nightfall she couldn't sleep. Sometimes she threw pillows at people. Yet doctors could find nothing wrong with her body. Many of them thought she was faking.

This was the shape she was in when Dr. Breuer first saw her. There was one cure for her that had not been tried—hypnosis. Other doctors had cured people with it. First they would hypnotize the patient. Then they would tell the patient not to be sick again.

Dr. Breuer started the hypnosis. "You are falling asleep. . ."

he said over and over. Soon Anna O was hypnotized.

"Is something bothering you?" he asked her.

Anna shook her head. She had no trouble turning her neck. Then she said something that made no sense. She said it in four languages, all in the same sentence. Breuer decided then not to tell her to get well. He wanted to see what went on in her mind.

Every day, he came over and hypnotized her. Then Anna would talk. She told him how she saw snakes—snakes that weren't there. She told him how people sometimes looked as if they were made of wax. The world in her hypnotized mind was frightening. But the talk seemed to make her better. She called it her "talking cure." She said she was sweeping out her mind.

She began to talk about things that happened when her father was sick. She told Breuer how she had not been able to see the watch. It upset her to tell about it. But after she came out from under hypnosis, her eyes were all right. They didn't blur any more.

She told about the snake behind her father's bed. Telling about it cured her arm. She could move it again.

And so it went on. It was as though she had two minds. One mind was in control when she was awake. The other,

when she was hypnotized, showed her hidden feelings. Telling feelings helped her to get well.

Anna was the first patient to undergo psychoanalysis. In a way, she and Dr. Breuer found it together. Before then, sickness of the mind was treated by food or drugs, or by giving shocks. It was Breuer and Anna who changed all that. What they did was discover a way to treat people with sick minds. It is called psychoanalysis. Psychoanalysis is still a "talking cure." Many people get well when they undergo it.

READING QUESTIONS

Choose the best answer. Write in your notebook the number of each question and the letter—a, b, c, d—that shows the best answer.

1. Which of the following titles best fits the story?
   (a) The Life Story of Dr. Breuer
   (b) The Uses of Hypnosis in Medicine
   (c) The Beginning of Psychoanalysis
   (d) How Anna O. Got Married

2. When did Anna get sick?
   (a) 1760
   (b) 1880
   (c) 1910
   (d) 1946

3. What was one of the things Anna was doing when she got sick?
   (a) Sweeping the house
   (b) Killing snakes
   (c) Taking care of her father
   (d) Cooking dinner

4. Why didn't Anna want her father to see her cry?
   (a) He would think she was a baby.
   (b) He would guess how sick he was.
   (c) She couldn't read the watch.
   (d) The doctor had told her it would be bad for him.

5. Why did Anna feel guilt when she fell asleep by her father's bed?
   (a) She was supposed to keep watch over him.
   (b) She never slept.
   (c) She had just had a nap.
   (d) It was wrong to sleep in a chair.

6. What did Dr. Breuer try with her?
    (a) Drugs
    (b) Plenty of sleep
    (c) A new place to live
    (d) Hypnosis

7. When did the problem with Anna's eyes begin?
    (a) When someone had hit her
    (b) When her tears blurred the watch face
    (c) When she was a baby
    (d) When she got a cold

8. How did Anna get well?
    (a) By tell her feelings
    (b) By throwing pillows
    (c) By eating oranges
    (d) By taking a vacation

WORDS TO KNOW

Choose the word that best fits the blank in each sentence. Write it in your notebook beside the number of the sentence.

patient   undergo   guilt   psychoanalysis

1. Anna O. was a _____ of Dr. Breuer.

2. Anna felt _____ for falling asleep.

3. One "talking cure" is called _____.

4. A person willing to _____ psychoanalysis might get well.

SPEAKING AND LISTENING

Discuss these questions with your classmates.

1. How did Anna O. have two minds? Which one ruled when she was awake? Which one ruled when she was

under hypnosis? Do you think all people have two minds? Why?

2. Psychoanalysis also deals with dreams. Dreams can tell a great deal about a person's hidden feelings. What dreams do you remember? Do you think they had anything to do with your hidden feelings? Why?

3. How might a person see something that really isn't there? Has anything ever looked like something else to you? What? Why might this have happened?

4. What do you think made Anna O. sick?

5. Has something in your mind—a worry, say—ever made you sick? How? Where do headaches come from? Why are you tired sometimes and not other times?

6. Have you ever been made suddenly afraid—such as a near hit by a car? What happened to your body? What does this tell you about mind and body?

FINDING IT

Find the city of Vienna on a map. Vienna is in Austria. Austria is in Europe.

WORDS THAT TELL ABOUT A KIND OF PERSON

What kind of person was Anna O.? You might say she was clever, or kind. In the story, find two sentences that tell she was clever. Write them on a separate piece of paper under the heading *Clever*. Now find three sentences, all together, that tell Anna was kind. Write them on the paper under the heading *Kind*.

NOTE: In later life, Anna O. turned out to be clever. She was a writer. And she was kind. She spent her life helping others.

For example, she started a home for poor children. Her real name was Bertha Pappenheim (BER-thuh PAP-un-hiem).

WRITING ABOUT DREAMS

On a piece of paper, draw a picture of a dream you had. Under the picture, write two or more sentences telling about the dream.

ROLLING THUNDER, MEDICINE MAN

Rolling Thunder is a Native American medicine man. There have been Native American medicine men for more than 2,000 years. They know how to cure sick people. What are their secrets?

When a Native American is about twelve years old, he goes into the mountains. It is his way of finding out what he will do with his life. With him, he takes only a blanket.

He takes no food and no water. For three days, he stays alone. He sees no one. During that time, he has a vision. The vision tells him what he will do with his life. Sometimes the vision is hard to figure out. When the boy comes down from the mountain, he tells a medicine man about the vision. The medicine man tells him what it means. Some boys have visions telling them to be medicine men.

Of course, that is only the beginning. Learning to be a medicine man takes time—eight years. During that time, the boy learns which plants cure people. He learns chants to say over sick people. He learns how to lay hands on the sick, and more. Native American medicine is not simple.

Native American medicine is based on a belief that people are part of nature. Things in nature must balance. If things are out of balance, people get sick. Because everything is part of everything else, when the land is sick, the people are sick.

Medicine men use several things when treating people

who are sick: a feather with a handle, a pipe, old chants. Here is one of the chants:

"To the East where the Sun rises.

To the North where the cold comes from.

To the South where the light comes from.

To the West where the sun sets.

To the Father Sun.

To the Mother Earth."

During this chant, the medicine man draws smoke from the pipe and blows it out four times: once when he faces east, once when he faces north, once when he faces south, once when he faces west.

Rolling Thunder is a medicine man. He works on the railroad. He also cures sick people. On his head he often wears a hat with feathers stuck in it. Once a rich man flew in a plane to see Rolling Thunder. He had some red

bumps on his back. He told Rolling Thunder he would pay him $10,000 to cure those bumps.

"Can you cure me?" he asked.

"Yes, I can cure you." said Rolling Thunder.

"Well, will you?"

"No, not now," said Rolling Thunder. He told the man to come back in a year. He told him to bring tobacco for his helpers and to talk to them first. And he told the man to take back his offer of the $10,000. Medicine men, said Rolling Thunder, can not be bought.

Native American medicine works a lot of the time. It works because medicine men know about plants, nature, and the powers of mind. There may be even more to it than that. Medicine men will not tell all their secrets.

READING QUESTIONS

Choose the best answer. Write in your notebook the number of each question and the letter—a, b, c, d—that shows the best answer.

1. What is this story mostly about?
   (a) Plants that cure people
   (b) The things medicine men do
   (c) Visions that some Native Americans have
   (d) The way some Native Americans keep secrets

2. How does a person become a medicine man?
   (a) He goes to school for it.
   (b) He is trained by a medicine man.
   (c) He is born to it.
   (d) He is chosen by the chief.

3. When does a Native American find out what he will do with his life?
   (a) When he is born
   (b) When he is about six

(c) When he is about twelve

(d) When he is about twenty

4. When does a Native American boy have the vision that determines his life?

(a) When he is alone in the mountains for three days

(b) When the medicine man tells him to have it

(c) When he is sick

(d) When he is put to sleep

5. What is one of the things a medicine man studies?

(a) Sailing

(b) Plants

(c) Woodworking

(d) Weaving

6. What do medicine men use when treating sick people?

(a) Warm blankets and soup

(b) A feather with a handle and a pipe

(c) A book and a candle

(d) A black bag and lotion

7. What does Rolling Thunder do when he is not acting as a medicine man?

(a) He teaches school.

(b) He writes for a magazine.

(c) He works on the railroad.

(d) He runs a store.

8. Why did the rich man come to see Rolling Thunder?

(a) To pay him $10,000

(b) To have Rolling Thunder cure some red bumps

(c) To hear Rolling Thunder's chants

(d) To learn how to paint

WORDS TO KNOW

Choose the word that best fits the blank in each sentence. Write it in your notebook beside the number of the sentence.

vision   chant   balance   medicine

1. Rolling Thunder is a _____ man.

2. Everything in nature should _____.

3. After three days on the mountain, he had a _____ telling him what he would do with his life.

4. Rolling Thunder sang the _____ while he smoked the pipe.

SPEAKING AND LISTENING

Discuss these questions with your classmates.

1. Some people go into the mountains to decide what they will do with their lives. How do you choose what you will do with your life?

2. What does Rolling Thunder think about man and nature? Do you agree? Why?

3. "When the land is sick, the people are sick." How do you feel about that sentence? In what real ways might it be true?

4. What might a medical doctor say about Rolling Thunder's medicine? Why?

RHYMING WORDS

By knowing about rhyming, you will find it easier to read new words. For example, if you know how to say the word *plant*, it is easy to figure out how to say the word *chant*.

Write the following pairs of sentences on a separate piece

of paper. In the blank in each second sentence, write a word that rhymes with the italicized word in each first sentence. The word you write should make sense in the sentence.

Example: The *plant* was poison.

The medicine man sang the *chant.*

1. Rolling Thunder is a medicine *man.*

   He _____ cure sick people.

2. When the earth is *sick,* the people are sick.

   Native American medicine is not a _____.

3. For three days, he stays *alone.*

   The chant is sung all on one _____.

4. The vision tells him what he will do with his *life.*

   Maybe he will get married and have a _____.

5. Most jobs take time to *learn.*

   When you can do something well, you can usually _____ money at it.

6. Medicine men use a *feather* with a handle.

   The _____ report says we will have a storm tomorrow.

7. He *blows* out the smoke four times.

   This plant _____ ten feet tall.

8. The rich man came in a *plane.*

   When his leg was hurt, he used a _____.

9. Part of the cure takes place in the *mind.*

   We cannot _____ out all the secrets of Indian medicine.

FINDING OUT FROM OTHERS

People for a long time have had simple ways of curing sick people. These ways are called folk medicine. Many of these ways work. Others don't. Ask an old person in your family about some of these ways. Find out from a book or a nurse or doctor if they work. Share them with the class.

THINKING ABOUT CAUSE AND EFFECT

Some people say everything is part of a chain. Everything is a result of something. And everything is a cause of something else.

Below are two lists. One is a list of causes. The other is a list of effects. Write the lists next to each other on a piece of paper. Then draw a line to match each cause to its effect.

Causes

A germ gets into your body.

Air gets in the car's gas line.

She told a lie.

He worked very hard.

She got stuck with a pin.

Effects

He earned a lot of money.

She cried with pain.

You get sick.

The car stops.

No one believed her any more.

WRITING ABOUT CAUSE AND EFFECT

Choose two pairs of causes and effects from the lists you matched on page 226. Combine each pair into one sentence. Write the sentence in your notebook. In each sentence link the cause with its effect.

Example:

cause	He worked very hard.
effect	He earned a lot of money.
one sentence	He worked very hard, and he earned a lot of money.

ROBOTS

WORDS

computers [kum-PEW-turz] machines that make fast mathematical
calculations

factory [FAK-tree] a place where things are made

sensors [SENS-erz] things that detect heat and light, among other
things, and can send signals

For a long time, inventors have been making machines that do
things on their own. These machines are called robots. Robots
can work without talking back to the boss. Robots don't ask for
raises. They do the same job the same way every time. Now
people are making robots that can do many different things.

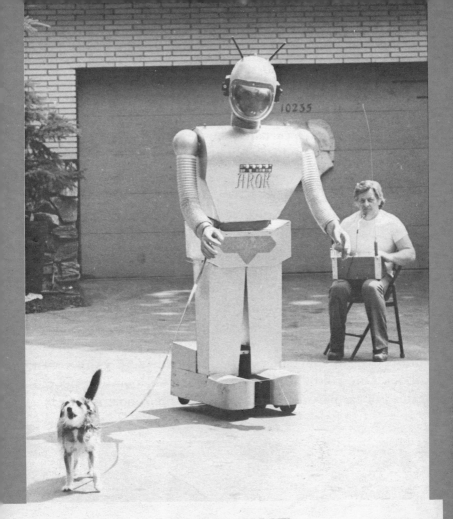

WHAT IS A ROBOT?

A thermostat is a robot. When it gets too cold, a thermostat can turn on the heat. When it gets too hot, a thermostat can turn off the heat. This robot can make two decisions—when to turn the heat on and when to turn it off.

Today, people make robots that contain computers. These robots can be set to make many different "decisions." They may also contain sensors that detect light, sound, movement, smell, touch, and heat.

For the fun of it, people have made some robots that look like human beings. But robots are not human. A robot is set by people to do a certain task when it gets a certain signal. A robot always has to do what it has been told to do.

ROBOTS IN THE FACTORY

Some robots are used in factories. Some are bolted to the floor. Others move around. Most are run by electricity. Factory robots can be set to pick up eggs or red-hot pieces of metal. They do jobs that people can't or won't do. They can be made to spray paint. They can put things in piles. They can pack boxes. One owner of a factory robot said, "The robot doesn't have coffee breaks. You talk to the robot, and it just keeps working. It just keeps running 24 hours a day." But robots are not perfect. Sometimes things go wrong with robots. One robot broke down. It started painting people instead of car parts. Workers get to like the robots. At one fac-

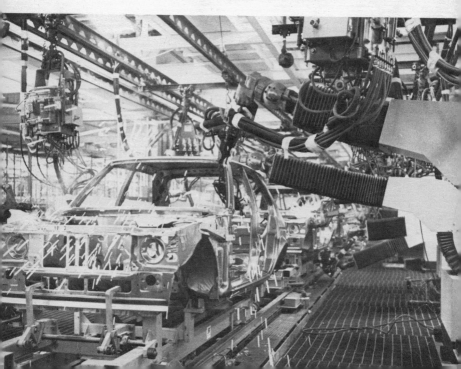

tory, when the robot Clyde the Claw broke down, the workers sent it flowers.

SIM

Sim looks like a person. Sim is a robot planned to act like a sick person. Students learning to be doctors practice on Sim. That way their mistakes won't hurt real people. If a doctor puts a needle in the wrong place in Sim's arm, the arm jerks. Sim acts as though it were in pain. If a doctor makes a very bad mistake, Sim even seems to die.

ROBOT FIREFIGHTERS

The robot firefighter is six feet tall. It weighs 1,300 pounds. In its chest is a hose to put out fires. Its ears are two lights. It has wheels and can climb stairs. Heat doesn't bother it. It can walk through fire.

CENTURY ONE

Century One is a guard robot. It is seven feet tall. At night it guards empty stores. If someone breaks in, its sensors pick up on the person's body heat. Century One locks in on the person. It gets to within eight feet of the person and the shouts "Stop." If the person keeps moving, Century One starts acting. It can send out a high sound that makes people's ears hurt. It can flash on a bright light that blinds people. It can gas them. Bullets bounce off Century One. Century One is not a thing to fool with.

HARDIMAN

Hardiman is a walking truck robot. Inside Hardiman is a person, who runs the robot. Hardiman can pick things up. When Hardiman picks up 1,500 pounds, it "feels" like 60 pounds to the person running it.

FUTURE ROBOTS

Robots are going to do even more in the future. You may have a robot of your own. It will clean for you. It will tape TV shows for you. When you want facts, your robot will flash them on a TV screen for you. Your robot's computer brain will probably be kept in a closet. You will be able to tell it what to do in English. It will be able to know what you have said. It will then do what you ask.

Some robots will be able to put machines together. Others will be sent out into space where they will work for a few years and then stop. Robots of the future may be able to think for themselves.

We may have robot judges. Imagine this. A person breaks into an empty store. The person is stopped by Century One. Then the person ends up in front of a judge robot who gives out a ten-year sentence. Who will be running the world then? People or robots?

READING QUESTIONS

Choose the best answer. Write in your notebook the number of each question and the letter—a, b, c, d—that shows the best answer.

1. What is this story mostly about?
    (a) Robots that go to the moon
    (b) New kinds of robots
    (c) The way robots move
    (d) How robots learn

2. What makes new robots different from those in the past?
    (a) They are made of metal.
    (b) They can do work.
    (c) They can make more "decisions."
    (d) They can respond to heat.

3. What usually gives power to robots?
    (a) Computers
    (b) Lights
    (c) Sensors
    (d) Electricity

4. What did workers do when Clyde the Claw broke down?
    (a) They broke him up.
    (b) They laughed.
    (c) They sent him flowers.
    (d) They painted him.

5. What part does Sim play?
    (a) A doctor
    (b) A sick person
    (c) A guard
    (d) A firefighter

6. What does Century One detect when someone breaks in?
   (a) Body heat
   (b) Footsteps
   (c) Doors opening
   (d) Smell

7. What does Century One do right after it locks in on the person?
   (a) It shouts "Stop!"
   (b) It shoots its gun.
   (c) It makes a phone call.
   (d) It gases the person.

8. What is Hardiman?
   (a) A robot firefighter
   (b) A computer
   (c) A walking truck
   (d) A person

WORDS TO KNOW

Choose the word that best fits the blank in each sentence. Write it in your notebook beside the number of the sentence.

sensors   factory   computers

1. Clyde the Claw was a _____ robot.

2. Through their _____ some robots detect body heat.

3. Robots use _____ to make decisions.

SPEAKING AND LISTENING

Discuss these questions with your classmates.

1. How is a robot different from a person? How is a robot like a person?

2. What jobs might robots *not* be able to do now?
   What jobs can robots do that people can't?

3. How does a robot see, hear, feel, and think? How does
   a person see, hear, feel, and think? If a robot did not
   have a computer brain, would it matter what it saw?
   Why? What part does your brain play in figuring out
   what you see and hear?

4. Will robots of the future be more like people? Why?

5. What might robots of the future do?

6. Read the last two sentences of the story again. What do
   they mean? What do you think about this idea?

WORDS THAT LOOK ALIKE BUT MEAN DIFFERENT THINGS

The word raise has at least two different meanings. One
meaning is "more money." For example, when people get
raises, they get more money in their paychecks. Another
meaning is "to lift." You use this meaning when you talk about
raising your hand to answer a question.

Write the following sentences and meanings on a separate piece of paper. For each italicized word, choose the correct meaning from the choices written below. Circle the
correct meaning.

1. *Light* came in through the window.
   (a) Pale
   (b) Something that makes it possible to see

2. New robots don't look much *like* people.
   (a) The same as
   (b) Care for

3. She asked him to *hand* her the shovel.
   (a) Give with the hand
   (b) Part of the body at the end of the arm

4. Factory robots *can* pick up an egg.
    (a) Are able to
    (b) Something that holds something else
5. Sim *acts* like a sick person.
    (a) Parts of plays
    (b) Behaves

DRAWING A CARTOON STRIP

On a piece of paper, draw a cartoon strip showing a robot. You might choose Century One stopping someone for coming into an empty store. You might choose Sim being worked on by a very bad student doctor. Or try one of your own ideas.

INTERVIEWING

With a friend, act out an interview. You be a person who works for a newspaper. Have your friend play a robot—the first robot that can really think for itself and talk. Before you begin the interview, write down some questions to ask. Here are some examples: "What do you think of people?" "What will you do now that you can think for yourself?" Take notes during the interview about the "robot's" answers.

WRITING A STORY

On a piece of paper, write a short story about a person and his or her robot. The story does not have to be very long. Four or five sentences will be enough. To get started, think about these questions:

1. How might a person feel about a robot?
2. How might a robot help a person?
3. Where might a robot go wrong?
4. Can a robot save a life? How?